# THE ESSENCE OF FAITH

# THE ESSENCE OF FAITH

## Philosophy of Religion

Albert Schweitzer

Translated and edited, and with a Foreword, by
Kurt F. Leidecker

Philosophical Library
New York

This study is based on Kantian metaphysics, from *The Critique of Pure Reason* to *Religion Within the Limits of Reason Alone.*

Printed in the United States of America.

*Distributed to the Trade by*
BOOK SALES, INC.
352 Park Avenue South
New York, N.Y., 10010

# Foreword

Kant's philosophy of religion, his religiosity and his concern with religion in general and Christianity in particular, have been treated by many, favorably as well as critically. They usually take Kant's biography as a background and search minutely the writings of his which discuss religious topics.

Such a routine job of producing just another exposition or review was certainly not to the liking of the young Albert Schweitzer in his doctoral thesis. He wanted to come closer to Kant's mind and to the sources of his motivation. This precluded somewhat a systematic presentation of Kant's ideas of religion and the philosophy of religion. More than that, it turned out that such a method would endanger the reputation of Kant as the most consistent and systematic thinker on all fronts.

This was not a matter of regret or something to be shied away from by the one who was to become the sage of Lambaréné. Quite the contrary. His secret delight over having discovered a deep affinity with Kant the moral genius is but thinly veiled in the often tedious and repetitious discussion in the true style of German philosophic tradition.

There is a sense of the noumenal in Schweitzer's life and thought. It saturates his mission of mercy, his reverence for life in any form, his devotion to Bach, his longing for fuller being. But it did not lead him to peaks of solitude; it led him to intensified social action. For, the noumenal with him is the moral, the total ethical commitment which is so profound it takes the place of religion. It is this same quality which he discovered in Kant's attempts and projects relating to a philosophy of religion as compared with the execution of his plans, marred by either the assimilation to the critical philosophy or the independent development of it.

It has rightly been said that the German phrase *Ehrfurcht vor dem Leben* means more than "reverence for life." It injects the flavor of holiness, sanctity, as well as gripping and awesome profundity in its realization. It is this attitude which Schweitzer manifested all his life. He discovered it in Kant as a moral genius.

Few who are, likewise, profoundly committed to either morality or religion extricate themselves from overwhelming mystical emotions and inarticulate gropings to master the language of reason and logic. Schweitzer did master the critical idealism of Kant, in fact he seems to imitate the involved style of the *Critiques*. He was exceedingly convinced that Kant was a profoundly moral genius, first and last, who developed a critical philosophy, rather than an intellectual *Allzermalmer* (all-destroyer) who made room for practical morality and religion only for the sake of expediency. Schweitzer crushes with utter logic many of the statements which Kant thought would favor his argument, but he assures us that it is for the glory of Kant the moral genius *par excellence*. The absolutely consistent Schopenhauer, who followed out the critical arguments of Kant relentlessly, is less esteemed by Schweitzer than the inconsistent Kant whose whole being identified itself with the moral ground of the universe.

This early masterpiece of dialectics and logic is important in that it shows up flaws in Kant's thinking, but more important in that it exhibits one side of Kant which is also the secret source of Schweitzer's genius and success.

KURT F. LEIDECKER

*Mary Washington College of*
*The University of Virginia*

# Contents

# Preface

◱ The present treatise seeks its justification in the following. It does not aim to be a work on Kant's philosophy of religion and it does not intend to pronounce a judgment. Rather, its purpose is to provide an opportunity for Kant to be heard once more after all the books that have been written about Kant's philosophy of religion. Therefore, this treatise offers, in the main, a critical analysis of Kant's thoughts in so far as they have some bearing on the problem of a philosophy of religion. This undertaking is not superfluous, but whether it has scientific significance is not for the author to decide.

For the present we have to avoid only one misunderstanding. The following analysis of those sections in the main works of Kant dealing with the philosophy of religion to some extent distorts the usual picture of Kant's philosophy of religion in some of its characteristics. It gains in wealth of ideas but, in turn, loses unity and completeness. The different stages of development in Kant's philosophy of religion will be drawn in bolder strokes than is usually the case. However, it would be wrong to assume that this presentation of Kant's philosophy of religion will displace the image drawn within the framework of general investigations of the philosophy of religion because it may be found to be more in keeping with the historical development of the various features. You really can no longer analyze and describe the Kantian philosophy of religion which has given direction to the development of the philosophy of religion in the 19th century, for it has already been portrayed in a masterly fashion by Kuno Fischer. We might define it as the philosophy of religion of Kant, oriented to the basic concepts of the *Critique of Practical Reason.* However, Kant's philosophy of religion, as it appears in our analysis of those of his writings which concern themselves with the philosophy of religion, has exercised hardly any influence on the 19th century. What value, then, does this portrayal have?

From the outset, it would seem that the interest in pointing up the true situation, which has been covered up by the state of things in their historic effectiveness, is very mild. Nevertheless, quite a different significance can be attached to such an undertaking, provided one reasons as follows. Kant's philosophy of religion has passed through a sizeable evolution. This development is necessarily orderly. If, now, we were able to recognize the laws of this development, would it, then, not be reasonable to assume that these laws will prove to be identical with the laws to which the philosophy of religion was subjected in the 19th century? The problem stated differently is whether the development of Kant's philosophy of religion is not in a certain sense a preformation of the development of the philosophy of religion in the 19th century.

A. SCHWEITZER

*Strassburg, December 1899*

# Introduction

Kant's philosophy of religion is an attempt to construct, with the aid of his own formulation of the moral law, a philosophy of religion on the basis of critical idealism as developed in the *Critique of Pure Reason*. To the extent that all writings following the *Critique of Pure Reason* refer in some way, be it more or less directly or obliquely, also to the significance of critical idealism for a philosophy of religion, a presentation of the Kantian philosophy of religion must, therefore, include that critique in its consideration. The question now before us is whether we should set down the individual trends of thought in the various writings indiscriminately in a general schematism of Kant's philosophy of religion such as would result from a combination of a philosophy of religion with critical idealism and, at the same time, utilize these individual characteristics in sketching a unified picture, or, whether the trends of thought in the philosophy of religion in the different writings, each considered by itself, already do represent sketches with respect to which it is a question whether they can be joined together in a unified picture. Attention to the latter possibility recommends itself easily in planning and executing an investigation into Kant's philosophy of religion for the sake of making as few assumptions as possible in the presentation. For, if the investigation proceeds along the path first mentioned and thoughts are detached from their intimate contexts without regard to the latter to be incorporated in the general plan of Kant's philosophy of religion, the presupposition is already implied that Kant's philosophy of religion does have a unified infrapattern into whose structure every thought respecting the philosophy of religion in the postcritical writings may be fitted.

Apart from this merely theoretical consideration still other circumstances speak in favor of the adoption of the second method. Some indications, indeed, point to the fact that a unified presentation of Kant's philosophy of religion must meet with difficulties if one does not choose to master all propositions concerning the philosophy of religion in accordance with the blueprint and the ideas contained in the *Critique of Practical Reason*. These difficulties appear as soon as one pursues one of the main concepts of Kant's philosophy of religion in respect to its occurence and significance in the course of the different Kantian treatments similar to what P. Lorentz did in the case of the concept of postulate in that he pointed out the variations, number, arrangement and formulation of the postulates.

⊐⅃ No matter with what concept of Kant's philosophy of religion one starts, all sorts of circumstances and problems may be singled out—without going into an investigation of how the thoughts are intertwined—as supporting a call for first devoting in such a presentation of Kant's philosophy of religion a special investigation to the individual trends of thinking in the different writings before proceeding to bring them together into a unified whole. This method is more circuitous and difficult than the one ordinarily employed . . . but it is amply compensated for by the fact that such an investigation is most intimately connected with the objective underlying every consideration of Kant's philosophy of religion, that is, the answer to the question whether or not critical idealism has succeeded in supporting a philosophy of religion. . . . Hence, the pattern for the investigation we are about to commence is justifiably established and presented as having its roots in the ultimate concern of every investigation of Kant's philosophy of religion.

# The Sketch of a Philosophy of Religion in the *Critique of Pure Reason*

T HE DESIGNATION of "sketch of a philosophy of religion" for that section of the *Critique of Reason* in which moral and religious interests are detectable in Kant's thinking is justified by the kind of presentation Kant makes. On pp. 605 ff.* of the canon of pure reason there is, indeed, a somewhat sketchy presentation of the thoughts which appear in a purely side-by-side arrangement, without exhibiting the unity of the *Critique of Pure Reason*. The concept of the postulate, the definition of religion, the comprehensive justification of the autonomy of the moral law, and the related and deeply probing treatment of the problem of freedom have not been attained here. The whole section merely forms the conclusion of the critical investigation concerning the limits of human knowledge; it treats the practical use of pure reason, in distinction from the speculative use. Nevertheless, it is just by

* Schweitzer's page references are to the Ph. Reclam edition, K. Kehrbach, editor.

virtue of this close connection with the investigations of critical idealism that this sketch of a philosophy of religion becomes valuable for the portrayal of the philosophy of religion in critical idealism.

The section of the *Critique of Pure Reason* dealing with the philosophy of religion offers, though perhaps only in outlines, the most consistent presentation of Kant's philosophy of religion in so far as it is the philosophy of religion of "critical idealism." Is it, then, correct to say that the development of the thought in this sketch of a philosophy of religion corresponds to the projected philosophy of religion of critical idealism as announced in the investigations of the *Critique of Pure Reason?* Is the outline of the sketch of a philosophy of religion identical with the outlines of a philosophy of religion in the transcendental dialectic in so far as the latter intends to lay the groundwork for a sketch of a philosophy of religion?

The practical use of reason leads us into the realm of morals and religion. Critical idealism furnishes the matter for the transcendental hypotheses which demonstrate the possibility of the ideas of reason. Thus, in the interrelationship of transcendental hypotheses with the assumptions of reason for practical purposes, there lies, at the same time, the relation of critical idealism to the philosophy of religion which is based on it. The ideas which are realized in the practical realm are prepared for this task by the instrumentality of critical idealism. They have moved into a sort of position of equilibrium, from which reason, employed practically, then pulls them toward its own realm. This relationship is also expressed in Kant's terminology;

he speaks, in this connection, of a *theoretical* (speculative) and a *practical* use of pure reason, yet does not distinguish —as he does later in the *Critique of Practical Reason*— between the two. This terminological distinction is grounded in a difference in thinking.

Very instructive is a footnote in the second edition of the *Critique of Pure Reason* where Kant connects the psychological, cosmological, and theological ideas with the ideas of God, freedom, and immortality, after developing them in the sequence of their later dialectical treatment: "Metaphysics has only three ideas as the true object of its search: God, freedom and immortality, understood so that the second concept in combination with the first should lead to the third as the necessary conclusion. Everything else with which this science occupies itself serves it only as a means to attain these ideas and their reality. It needs them not for the sake of natural science, but in order to transcend nature. Insight into them would make theology, morality, and (by combining the two) religion, and, hence, the highest aims of our existence dependent merely on the speculative faculty of reason, and nothing else. In a systematic presentation of these ideas, the order, as given, would be the most appropriate one, being synthetic. However, in the preliminary treatment which is necessary, the analytical presentation which reverses this order will be more appropriate, so that we may, proceeding from what experience presents us with immediately—that is, from psychology to cosmology and, hence, to the knowledge of God—realize our grand design" (p. 290). This passage is most important for the problem confronting us.

With the treatment of the problem of freedom we have reached the point where the positive exposition of the sketch of a philosophy of religion begins to clearly stand out from the outlines of our transitional thinking. We have presented the latter up till now in their most general formulation so as to be able to survey the thinking by which the *Critique of Pure Reason* arrives from its critical labor at those sections which have reference to the practical realization of the three ideas of God, freedom and immortality.

Let us summarize the essential points of the investigation thus far. The keynote of the transitional thoughts comes to the fore in Kant's use of language. By the expressions "pure reason in theoretical usage" and "pure reason in practical usage," he is indicating that at this juncture the absolute unity of reason is much more strongly than at any time later the presupposition of his thinking. At the same time, we are given to understand that his thoughts about the philosophy of religion advance here on the presupposition that the "ideas" which reason realizes in its practical use are absolutely identical with the ideas to which reason in its theoretical employment had been driven as it advanced of necessity from the conditioned to the unconditioned. Overcoming skepticism is the point from which the transitional thoughts we have noted start. With this, we have expressed the basic thought of the sketch of the philosophy of religion in the transcendental dialectic. This now obligates us to clearly expound how, from the number of the ideas treated, the three ideas have developed which are realized later practically, that is, how they specifically attained a practical religious value.

Kant is cautious and reticent when he applies the term "idea" to the individual subjects treated in the cosmological discussions. On p. 345, he specifically speaks of four cosmological ideas: "There are, therefore, not more than four cosmological ideas, according to the four headings of the categories." The linguistic expression regarding the term idea is pursued consistently only for the concept of freedom. (The reasons for and the significance of this fact will occupy us shortly.) Kant remains consistent, however, in his thought heralded by the designation "system of cosmological ideas," in that he retains the cosmological ideas in systematic connection in those sections where, from the standpoint of the practical use of reason, interest in the thoughts treated in the cosmological dispute is illuminated. The clearest expression of this systematic connection may be found in those lines which designate the decisive turning point at which the cosmological ideas move into the spotlight of reason in its practical use.*

What interest does reason have for the "thesis" in question in the cosmological dispute? "First of all, a certain practical interest which every right-thinking person shares heartily if he looks out for his real advantage. That the world has a beginning, that my thinking self is of a simple and, therefore, indestructible nature, that this self is, at the same time, free in its spontaneous actions and beyond natural necessity, and that, finally, the whole order of things which constitute the world are derived from some original Being from whom everything borrows its unity and purposeful connection—these are so many foundation stones of morality and religion."

* These lines, which are of decisive importance, are found on p. 385.

In order to appreciate the entire significance of these lines, one must again and again remind oneself of the fact that we are dealing here with a section in which Kant stresses only the practical value of the cosmological thoughts, not that of the problems treated generally in the dialectic. Here we are merely concerned with the "system of cosmological ideas." All four antinomies are represented, all four are evaluated practically, and all four stand in that particular context in which they had been treated previously dialectically. Simultaneously with this practical evaluation they were subjected to a deflection from their generality in the direction of their formulation with reference to the knowing subject.

What significance do the antinomies have for the ethical and religious view of the world of the knowing subject which sees through their dialectical appearance?

The first antinomy is most thoroughly opposed to this new orientation: "The world has a beginning in time and is, furthermore, limited in regard to space" (p. 354). Even in the dialectical treatment, this first antinomy looks somewhat strange. One has the impression that the dialectic would not suffer if this antinomy had been kept from us. Its subordinate place appears at the instant the transcendental ideas move toward the realm of reason in its practical use. It loses half of its scope in that it only retains its temporal character while it has lost its connection with space. "That the world has a beginning, . . . is a foundation stone of morals and religion" (p. 385). In this abbreviated form, where the stiltedness of the connection of the first cosmological idea with the thought of the conclusion is clearly apparent, we see that the first cosmological idea is dragged onto the new field only because of its systematic connection with the rest of the ideas. The mutilation which it suffers thereby, and the unaccustomed atmosphere of the practical use of reason, accelerate its inevitable end. Exhausted, it collapses. In what follows, not even its demise is announced. It is the fate of every artificial existence.

In the practical ramifications of the cosmological antinomies which extend through several sections (pp. 382-451), the main interest is taken up by the idea of freedom which is treated therein. The central position which this idea occupies in Kant's philosophy in general and in his philosophy of religion in particular comes clearly to the fore. Nowhere has any idea been so fully prepared with respect to its practical realization as the idea of freedom has been in this case. This is already indicated in the frequent use of the word "idea" in application to the concept of freedom treated here, while, for the rest, the application of this term to the theses of the "system of cosmological ideas" remains rather limited. It is quite characteristic for the correctness of the previous investigation that Kant refers to freedom in this connection now as a "transcendental idea," and then again as a "cosmological idea," without indicating that the latter designation really ought to stand in a subordinate relationship to the former. This idea of freedom is the only one which Kant developed to the point where it is about to experience its practical realization. It is exactly that idea which is discussed mainly in the *Critique of Practical Reason*. Thus, at the end of this investigation concerning the scheme of a philosophy of religion in the dialectic, it remains for us to briefly call to mind the preparation which the practical realization of the idea of freedom receives in the transitional sections of the second main portion of the second book of the dialectic in order to be able to decide, as we pass on to the sketch of the philosophy of religion, whether and to what extent the treatment and realization of the idea of freedom given on pp. 608 and 609 correspond to the anticipatory discussion which Kant offers us with regard to this problem.

The preliminary discussion of the practical realization of the idea of freedom takes place on pp. 428 to 445. In every respect, the discussions in these pages set forth the culmination of Kant's presentation of the dialectic. The whole investigation progresses in a highly effective crescendo.

First of all, Kant brings clarity to the problem that is raised here. What is the relationship between the idea of freedom in practical reason and the transcendental or cosmological idea of freedom when reason is used theoretically? By the first-mentioned, Kant understands "the independence of spontaneity from being necessitated by the promptings of sensibility" (p. 429). The last-mentioned has reference to the decision as to "whether causality in conformity to the laws of nature is the only causality or whether we have to assume an additional causality through freedom to explain it" (p. 368). If one were to adhere to the definition given here it would appear as if there were two ideas of freedom independent of each other of which the former does not depend on the latter for realization. However, on p. 385 the practical idea of freedom is already understood as that form which "the cosmological idea of freedom" assumes in its transition to the field of the practical use of reason. This relationship is again attested to on p. 429, and the circumstance is emphasized. And it is in this that Kant's thinking advances—that in this linkage of the two, the difficulty of the realization of the practical idea of freedom rests. "It is extremely noteworthy that the practical concept of freedom is based on this transcendental idea of freedom, and that the transcendental idea of freedom constitutes the really difficult factor in the practical concept, a circumstance which has surrounded the problem of its possibility ever since" (p. 429). We could designate this proposition as fundamental in Kant's treatment of the problem of freedom. Thus, the possibility of solving this difficulty is a matter solely for transcendental philosophy (p. 430). In all this, the insight of critical idealism into the character of the world of appearance offers the only starting point from where removal of the difficulty may be begun, "for if appearances are things-in-themselves, freedom cannot be salvaged" (p. 431). Hence, the cosmological idea of freedom can be presented by means of critical idealism in conjunction with a general "necessity" (p. 434), provided this connection can be justified at all. That the "cosmological idea of freedom" is treated here with a view to the practical idea of freedom is evident from the fact that the problem of the connection between freedom and the law of causality is no longer put in relationship at all with appearances, as it was in the third cosmological antinomy, but is related to the relationship of human action with the causality of appearances as was done on p. 385. Kant's statement here attains wonderful clarity: "Man is one of those appearances of the sensuous world and, hence, also one of the natural causes whose causality must be subject to empirical laws. As such, man must, therefore, also have an empirical character, just as all other things in nature. Man alone, who otherwise knows nature merely through his senses, knows himself also in mere apperception and, to be sure, in actions and inner determinations which he cannot count among the sense impressions at all. He is, let us acknowledge, on the one hand, a phenomenon for himself, but, on the other hand—and that in view of certain faculties—a mere intelligible object because his actions cannot be counted as receptivity of sensibility" (pp. 437 and 438). The kind of necessity expressed by the "ought" permits us to look upon the case as possible in itself that reason, in view of appearance, does possess causality (pp. 438 and 439). Concerning the actuality or possibility of this practical freedom, nothing can be stated if we consider it in its indissoluble relation to the transcendental idea of freedom. Only the fact "that nature is at least not struggling against the causality of freedom, was the only thing we were able to accomplish, showing which was what we had solely and merely in mind" (p. 445).

The scheme of a philosophy of religion in the transcendental dialectic consisted in procuring—as concerns the practical use of reason—practical reality for the speculative ideas of pure reason in so far as we are persuaded that its significance concerns the practical use of reason. The idea of freedom corresponds to the third cosmological idea. It has reference to "whether causality according to the laws of nature is the only one from which the appearances of this world can *in toto* be derived, or whether it is possible to assume, in addition, a causality through freedom." (cf. *Critique of Pure Reason*, p. 368). For a rational being, the problem thus stated holds interest because it depends for its solution on whether his actions may be explained only by the general law of causality according to the mechanism of nature into which they are, as phenomena, incorporated, or whether he can consider these same actions as a space-time explanation of intelligible facts which are free in so far as they concern the intelligible cause of our volition. The idea of freedom which tends toward practical realization—and so all we have said up to now may be summarized—is the transcendental idea of freedom which rests upon the relationship of the intelligible and the phenomenal world which critical idealism has demonstrated as possible.

This brief survey of the attempts which the Kantian philosophy of religion undertook for the purpose of realizing the moral idea of freedom with the aid of the presuppositions of critical idealism, shows that these attempts treat progressively more and more in depth all of the formulations which the problem of moral freedom can assume in continuous series, beginning with the sketch of a philosophy of religion, which has not even grasped yet the problem in its difficulty, to the investigation of the radical evil, where the problem turns out to be insoluble. For these formulations demand the investigation, with progressive understanding in depth, of the moral law in one form or another. Corresponding to this bolder appearance of the purely ethical interest of the problem of freedom, the idea of transcendental freedom recedes more and more in any combination of the transcendental and the practical ideas of freedom. Thus, in view of the problem of freedom, we have characterized the development of Kant's philosophy of religion as a progressive emphasis on the ethical element and a progressive recession of the material which critical idealism assembles for the structure. It is the idea of freedom which forms the basis of all statements in this connection. A displacement in the treatment of the idea of freedom has in its train the displacement of all thought relationship and the giving of a different coinage to all concepts rooted therein.

After this preview, which was necessary for an insight into the peculiarity and significance of the treatment of the idea of freedom in the practical use of reason given in the sketch of a philosophy of religion, we are resuming the train of thought of this sketch. In view of the practical use of reason in the trinity of ideas, the place of the idea of freedom, corresponding to the cosmological questions, has been taken by the idea of a practical reason which extends only to the field of human action. The idea of freedom which has thus been displaced returns later on in the thinking of this investigation, in that it displays a practical and moral interest in a general reference to the totality of appearances. It appears on the scene as "the practical idea of a moral world" (p. 612). Already, the introduction to this "practical idea of a moral world" has shown its affinity to the idea of a practical freedom. Its starting point is, namely, the fact of the moral law. "I assume that there are really pure moral laws which determine entirely *a priori* (without regard to empirical reasons, such as happiness) our commissions and omissions, that is, the use of freedom in general in a reasonable being, and that these laws make absolute demands (not merely hypothetical ones by presupposing other empirical ends), and hence are to all intents and purposes necessary" (p. 611).

In what follows (on p. 612), all the difficulties of the practical realization of the idea of freedom in the moral application return once again. If the moral law manifests itself as the principle in the events of human actions, they, as free actions, must demonstrate "a special kind of systematic unity, that is, the moral one" as a practical reality, "while the systematic unity of nature could not be proven according to the speculative principles of reason" (p. 612). The use of the term "principle" in these few lines bears witness to the difficulty which meets us here. First of all, Kant talks about "principles of the possibility of experience, not in the speculative, but in a certain practical, that is, the moral use of reason." Next, he is concerned with a "systematic unity of nature according to speculative principles of reason." Then, he is concerned with the "causality of the moral principles of reason." At last he speaks of "principles of pure reason in its practical, but especially in its moral use" (p. 612). The difficulties assert themselves much more strongly than on pp. 608 and 609. The solution remains the same. The realm of human actions is delineated from the realm of natural events and reduced to the free causality of reason, "because reason possesses causality, to be sure, in view of freedom in general, but not in view of nature as a whole, and moral principles of reason can produce, to be sure, free actions, but not natural laws."

In the present sketchy treatment of the idea of a practical realization of the moral concept of God, its real content is covered up by the concept of happiness which, obscured by the way in which it usually occurs in another train of thought, clouds the insight into the peculiarity of the thought connections that meet us here. The great importance which is to be attributed to the distinction of these two trains of thought in the investigation of Kant's philosophy of religion requires that we trace their outlines in this sketch of the philosophy of religion where they met us first in a still undeveloped form side by side, so as to gain an insight into their differences. The middle term, which seemingly equates them, is the concept of happiness. What is its place in the realization of the idea of God (p. 613 ff.)? In this case, the concept of a moral world is brought into relation with moral mankind in whom acting humanly and morally is thought of as the causal principle of happiness. In this concept of the moral world a perfect ethics is identical with a perfectly achieved happiness. The moral world is a "system of morality which is its own reward" (p. 613). The ethical onus of the individual person in the moral world thus interpreted has, therefore, as object procuring one's own and at the same time others' happiness by achieving perfect ethics. It is exactly for the purpose of maintaining the justification of the ethical onus thus understood, in spite of the anticipation that not all members of humanity who are meant to belong to the moral world will act in that way, that Kant proceeds toward the realization of the concept of God.

We are at the end of the first part of our investigation.

It is true, we have only dealt with the first two sections of the canon of pure reason which contains the sketch of a philosophy of religion, and it remains to investigate only the third section "Concerning Opinion, Knowledge and Faith" (pp. 620 to 628). However, this section is of less importance for an insight into Kant's philosophy of religion since, compared with the two first sections, it does not present any advance in thought at all. It offers thoughts which are lacking in correct and precise delineations. Its investigation holds interest for an understanding of Kant's philosophy of religion only if and when we attack the general question as to what relation the sketch of the philosophy of religion (the conclusion of which constitutes this third section) has to the scheme of a philosophy of religion in transcendental dialectics and to the entire critical undertaking in general. In view of the above quotation the significance of this section, "Concerning Opinion, Knowledge and Faith," rests on the fact that the thoughts contained therein have already occurred in a much clearer and deeper form in the transcendental dialectic. The entire critical undertaking of the dialetic has, as we all know, the one objective of destroying opinion and purifying knowledge. The scheme of a philosophy of religion in the dialectic seeks to explain the scope, justification, and nature of faith in so far as it is not merely compatible with purified knowledge, but is also required by it. Thus, this third section of the canon of pure reason looks like an anachronism. It becomes understandable as being justified only when one carves out the sketch of a philosophy of religion, the canon of pure reason, out of the great critical opus, and seeks to understand it purely in itself, without its connection with the scheme of a philosophy of religion of transcendental dialectics.

These brief remarks are meant merely to explain why we are not devoting a more extensive investigation to this third section of the sketch of a philosophy of religion. The problem for which it has meaning at all concerns the relationship of the sketch of a philosophy of religion to the transcendental dialectic. In the discussions thus far this problem has always been recognized as the main one and presented as such. Nevertheless, if, at the conclusion of the analytical discussions of Kant's presentation, we wish to decide the questions which have emerged in the course of the investigation, the main problem referred to above cannot be settled first.

Now that we are at the end of the quite onerous investigation, the whole situation appears to us as a system of concentric circles. The problem as to what, on the whole, the general character of Kant's philosophy of religion is in the *Critique of Pure Reason* represents the outer circle. The circle closely following inside has reference to the distinction between the scheme of a philosophy of religion in the dialectic and the scheme of the sketch of a philosophy of religion. Pursuing the narrowing-down process of the investigations further, we were first searching more deeply for the essence of the scheme of a philosophy of religion in the transcendental dialectic. Then we analyzed the arrays of thought in the sketch of a philosophy of religion. The circles became smaller and smaller. Within the sketch of a philosophy of religion itself two different thought-structures separated out. Our analytical investigation pursued their differentiation in so far as the fluctuating outlines permitted it. This undertaking, which forms the conclusion of the analytical investigation in general, presents itself as the innermost circle in the system of concentric circles. The path in the analytic investigations went from the outermost circle to the innermost one. In our concluding investigations and in the unified summarization of the thoughts dealt with, we shall go in an opposite direction and run from the inner to the outer circles.

We did arrange the two trends of thought of the sketch of a philosophy of religion side by side and attempted to draw them in sharp outlines. Oftentimes these outlines were drawn more sharply than Kant's fluctuating sketchy type of presentation seemed to permit. This procedure, however, could be justified by the fact that this sharply drawn side-by-side arrangement was made because of the following grand development of Kant's philosophy of religion. In the sketch of a philosophy of religion, the two great trains of thought which appear later in Kant's philosophy of religion are found side by side in a somewhat confused state. The train of thought characterized by us as "the first one" is wound up by the presentation of the "moral theology" in the *Critique of Judgment* and in *Religion Within the Limits of Reason Alone*. It is distinguished by virtue of the fact that our ethical interest in continuing our existence, be it in the form of a "future life" or as "immortality," recedes somewhat into the background, and in place of it, interest in our terrestrial existence assumes greater validity. The latter fact manifests itself in the greater depth to which the problem of ethical freedom is subjected in discussion. To this must be added the predominance of the ethical element in the formulation of the concept of God. The progress of the *Critique of Judgment* and of *Religion Within the Limits of Reason Alone*, compared with the first train of thought of the sketch of a philosophy of religion, rests upon the understanding of the ethical law, which becomes gradually and progressively deeper.

Let us now summarize the thoughts which pertain to the sketch of a philosophy of religion as we ponder them as a whole. They are interconnected by the tripartite disposition which is to be found on p. 610. Concerning freedom, it is asserted that the question as to transcendental freedom has nothing to do with practical freedom. This is possible only if we constantly keep in mind the more comprehensive concept of the practical use of pure reason which the sketch of a philosophy of religion presupposes. The wider scope of this concept is based on a comprehension of the facts of the moral law which has not yet attained the highest degree of ethical profundity. Correspondingly, also the ethical element often recedes, to our surprise, in both questions in which the theoretical and the practical interest of pure reason touch each other. Neither the formulation of the question as to the existence of God nor that as to our continued existence allows the moral interest to come to the fore sufficiently. Great significance is attributed in the sketch of a philosophy of religion to the teleological trends of thought by means of which the conviction as to the existence of God and of a future life is established to such an extent that we gain the impression at the conclusion of the third section that the moral certitude was only meant to neutralize certain inevitable fluctuations in doctrinal faith concerning these two questions.

In this summary the way has now been prepared for the decision regarding the problem on hand, that is, whether and in how far the development of thought in the sketch of a philosophy of religion corresponds to the scheme of a philosophy of religion in transcendental dialectics. The basic thoughts of the latter are still in our mind. The scheme rests on the unity of pure reason in its theoretical and practical use. Thus, we are supposed to procure for the "three" ideas the practical interest of the transcendental, or (according to p. 385) cosmological, ideas the right to exist in the realm of practical reason. This is to take place in this manner so that theoretical reason may guide the transcendental idea in question through all phases up to its limits where it is ready to transcend it (using a passport which documents its origin in the land of critical idealism) and to settle down in the realm of the practical use of pure reason. We were able to pursue the different phases as they move from the widest formulation of a transcendental idea to the definitive, practical, and moral form of one of the ideas in the scheme of three ideas only with respect to the development of the idea of freedom. It alone is being groomed for practical realization for us to see. Thus, it is above all characteristic for the scheme of a philosophy of religion in transcendental dialectics.

The basic thought behind this scheme concerning the idea of freedom rests upon the idea "that it is upon the transcendental idea of freedom that the practical concept of it is based and that the transcendental idea constitutes properly the difficult factor in the idea of freedom, a problem which has for a long time surrounded the question as to the possibility of freedom" (p. 429). All that this critical preparation of the practical idea of freedom by means of the transcendental idea of freedom is able to accomplish is to demonstrate that "nature at least does not run counter to causality from freedom" (p. 445).

The detailed investigation of the treatment of the problem of freedom in the sketch of a philosophy of religion on pp. 608 and 609 has shown that in this decisive problem the scheme of the philosophy of religion in transcendental dialectics has been completely broken down. The question as to transcendental freedom has been totally severed from the problem of practical freedom, while the development of transcendental dialectics on pp. 428 to 445 remains steadfast in the union of both in spite of the fact that it is precisely in this combination that the difficulty of the whole problem lies.

The final sentence with which the treatment of the idea of transcendental freedom finishes on p. 445 contains something pointing to the future: "That nature, at least, is not incompatible with causality through freedom, was the only thing we were able to accomplish and it was this and this alone we had in mind" (p. 445). Why this modesty and yet this confidence? Because now nothing stands in the way of practical freedom, in spite of its entanglement with the transcendental idea of freedom. But now we behold the spectacle that at the point where practical freedom steps on the scene it rejects all connection with the transcendental idea of freedom because the latter has nothing to do with anything practical!

God, freedom and a future life are designated now as "objects" (twice on pp. 604 and 605), now as "cardinal propositions" (p. 607), now as "problems" (p. 607) in the sketch of a philosophy of religion in the first section where they appear in this triune number. After freedom has been eliminated from this triad "because this problem does not belong to reason in its practical use" (p. 609), only "two problems remain" (p. 609). These two are designated in what follows ordinarily as problems (pp. 610 and 619), as concepts, as doctrines (p. 624), or as articles of faith (p. 627). The term "idea" occurs sixteen times, twice on p. 610, twice on pp. 611, 612, 613, three times on pp. 614 and 615, twice on pp. 616 and 617, and on pp. 619, 620, and 625. Of these, a number of passages have reference to the moral law in general. "Judging morality as to its purity and consequences is done according to ideas, adhering to its laws, according to maxims" (p. 615). "The moral law . . . is a mere idea" (p. 615). "In the practical idea moral disposition and happiness are united" (p. 616).

A second group of passages connects the term idea with the concept of a moral world. "The moral world is a mere, yet practical idea which can in actuality have an influence on the world of the senses in order to shape it as much as possible in accordance with it" (p. 612). (What is designated here as "practical idea" is something totally different from what is otherwise understood by "idea of pure reason for practical use.") "Morality and happiness are inseparably connected only in the idea of pure reason" (p. 613). "The system of a morality which is its own reward is only an idea" (p. 613). "The moral law can rest on mere ideas of pure reason and may be known *a priori*" (p. 611). "I call the idea of such an existence . . . which is the cause of all happiness in the world in so far as it stands in exact ratio to morality, the ideal of the highest good" (p. 614). "The world must be conceived as having sprung from an idea . . . if it is to be consonant with the moral use of reason which rests absolutely on the idea of a highest good" (p. 617).

We have arrived at the end of the final summation of our investigation. The main problem as to whether the sketch of a philosophy of religion, the moral-theological culmination of Kant's great critical opus, really presents the basic outlines of the philosophy of religion of critical idealism had to be denied because the development of the sketch of a philosophy of religion makes no reference at all to the scheme of a philosophy of religion in transcendental dialectics and does not presuppose any acquaintance with it at all. Hence, this sketch has, in the presentation of the philosophy of religion of critical idealism, as it is usually given in connection with the *Critique of Practical Reason*, no rightful place. However, if one considers Kant's philosophy of religion as a whole, taking account of the development which it has undergone up to *Religion Within the Limits of Reason Alone*, the sketch of a philosophy of religion does occupy an eminent place. It points to what is to come and contains the entire future development, as it were, in a nutshell. It combines trains of thought which are at odds with each other because their undeveloped form does not yet permit such a unification. Later on these two trains of thought develop fully and clearly and become distinct. They are kept together only by virtue of Kant's profound moral genius. In this way, research into Kant's philosophy of religion turns into a presentation of its development.

# The *Critique of Practical Reason*

⊒ The main problem remains the same as for the investigation into the sketch of a philosophy of religion. It is concerned with whether and in how far Kant's composition on the philosophy of religion, as we have dealt with it here, does correspond in its development to the scheme of a philosophy of religion in transcendental dialectics. The solution of this problem seems to assume, in the case of the *Critique of Practical Reason,* a more positive formulation than in respect of the sketch of a philosophy of religion. In the *Critique of Practical Reason* we really get an idea triad. The discussion concerning freedom demonstrates the sincerity and depth which the transcendental dialectic seems to demand. Furthermore, the three ideas stand in an organic connection with each other. And yet, precisely at the decisive moment, this agreement has not been maintained. To be sure, the result in the *Critique of Practical Reason* is the same as is likewise to be expected in the development of the scheme of a philosophy of religion in the transcendental dialectic. Still, the method displays a characteristic difference. According to the scheme of a philosophy of religion in the transcendental dialectic, the fact of the moral law serves to realize in practice the ideas which appear problematic in the field of the theoretic use of reason. In the *Critique of Practical Reason* the moral law generates by itself demands which constitute the possibility of the highest good. After practical reason has, from an inner necessity, attributed reality to these demands in practice, it realizes, in order to confirm, as it were, the correctness of its procedure, that these practically realizable magnitudes which belong to the possibility of the highest good are identical with the ideas which in the realm of theoretical reason were regarded as problematic.

One must not parallel the sketch of a philosophy of religion and the *Critique of Practical Reason* if one has in mind posing and solving the problem of freedom. Both have as little in common with each other as does the problem of freedom in practical use with the problem of transcendental freedom in the sketch of a philosophy of religion. While the latter starts entirely with a separation of both problems of freedom, and finds the solution in the fact that it presupposes this separation as self-evident, the *Critique of Practical Reason* has— in view of the problem of freedom —in common with the scheme of a philosophy of religion in the transcendental dialectic the fundamental presupposition that it assumes the two kinds of freedom as being in insoluble connection with each other. Furthermore, the *Critique of Practical Reason* shares with the transcendental dialectic the circumstance that the treatment of the problem of freedom turns into a profound struggle of ideas where one comes face to face not only with Kant the philosopher, but Kant the profoundly moral person.

As we investigate the realization of the idea of freedom in the *Critique of Practical Reason,* we witness the following peculiar spectacle. In seizing upon the problem (cf. p. 113), the presentation starts with the scheme of a philosophy of religion as laid down in the *Critique of Practical Reason.* The treatment proper and the realization of the idea of freedom (pp. 114-127) take place in the shape of a double polemic, first against empiricism (p. 114), then against the false teachers of metaphysics. The empiricists are charged with not recognizing the importance of the transcendental idea of freedom in practical freedom; the latter are charged with discrediting the idea of transcendental freedom because of their shortsightedness and, thus, of putting the moral idea of freedom in jeopardy against their will. In that the interest of the investigation is concentrated on the transcendental idea of freedom (according to the polemic tendency of the presentation), the scheme of a philosophy of religion in transcendental dialectic becomes operative spontaneously, as it were. After realizing the idea of freedom, this section concludes with a remark which embraces the scheme of a philosophy of religion of the *Critique of Practical Reason* and seems to presuppose that the realization of the idea of freedom has presently come about in accordance with it!

Let us look back upon the road travelled by us in our

investigation. The problem presented itself in view of the possibility of judging every individual act morally. The solution was made possible by virtue of the knowledge offered by critical idealism, according to which the individual act is to be looked upon as a phenomenon within the mechanism of nature, but as free in view of its intelligible character so far as the subject judging his own actions is concerned. The insight into the ideality of space and time (p. 118) served to lift every individual act out of its causal nexus (according to which it seemed necessary and apart from the realm of moral responsibility) and to remove it into the mode of viewing the appearance of freedom of a noumenon, whereby it could be judged morally in the self-consciousness of a rational being. The same reflection was then utilized on p. 120 in order to be able to explain the fact that we feel repentance over a past deed by lifting it out of the sequence of the causal nexus and judging it, freed, as it were, of the time relation, according to the absolute spontaneity of freedom—always, however, presupposing the identity of the acting and the judging subject!

Beginning with p. 120, this identity is cancelled while reflection trained on the double nature of the actions remains intact. With this, however, an entirely new approach is initiated. Up till then, actions were pursued in their two-sidedness in line with phenomena as well as in the intelligible sphere. In the center, and uniting both, stood the moral consciousness of the acting subject. From then on Kant emphasizes, aside from the two-sided nature of every individual act, also the orderly connection of the acts among themselves. If the actions appear in the world of phenomena—"which, on account of the uniformity of behavior, announce their natural connection"—in an orderly connection, then the question is whether the problem of freedom must not also lift the individual act out of this connection in order to be able to judge it morally. It is of decisive importance that the investigation abandons the presupposition of the identity of the judging subject and, at the same moment, the subject that is judged. In this reflection, the unity of judgment of an act is to be concentrated on only in so far as it manifests itself as a phenomenon under the mechanism of nature and as an intelligible act under the law of freedom. However, by virtue of the fact that all these preliminary presuppositions are unconsciously abandoned, one after another, the problem which we investigated became quite a different one, unnoticed. The resulting displacement becomes most pronounced in the displacement of the middle term which united the intelligible and the empirical mode of reflection. Previously, it had been the knowledge the intelligible self has of the moral law. Now, the place of the intelligible self, which is at the same time conscious of the moral law, has been taken by the moral character in so far as it expresses itself in regular acts which, on account of their uniformity of behavior, indicate a connection with nature. Earlier, the question was: How can I think of an act which, as phenomenon, is subsumed under the mechanical laws of nature, as having been effected at the same time under freedom, in so far as judging it is required, which the moral law urges upon me through my conscience? The answer is as follows: By virtue of the fact that space and time, in which this has taken place in conformity with the causality of phenomena so far as I understand and know it, have no application to my intelligible self and, consequently, my act also, in so far as it is merely an expression of my disposition which concerns the moral law, is to be judged by me not according to natural necessity (which would be proper to it as a phenomenon), but according to the absolute spontaneity of freedom.

Moral consciousness demands that every deed, in order to be able to be judged as moral, be looked upon as free. That the act which is judged morally is free, and is to be understood as a free effect of the subject from which it proceeds, is the presupposition which is at the basis of every moral judgment. With the progressive insight into the mechanism of nature, with the expansion of the concept "natural event" even into the realm of human actions, this presupposition has been shaken. With it also the moral law falters, since it has to turn out to be an illusion if freedom cannot be salvaged. Our moral consciousness rises in indignation against such a situation. With all means of science, with the expenditure of the greatest acumen to understand the nature of what happens, it seeks to find ways and means whereby the action to be judged morally may be lifted out of the course of natural events and understood as free. In that it attempts to understand scientifically the presupposition of every moral judgment, the epistemological problem attains its profound moral significance by which alone it legitimizes itself as belonging to "philosophy" in the more pregnant Kantian sense. At the same time, the epistemological problem, when perfectly grasped by critical idealism, exhibits a form which not only does not resist being related to the scientific justification of the presupposition of our moral judgment, but even demands it itself. In the reconciliation of contradictions by the transcendental idea of freedom, even the contradictions of the practical idea of freedom seem to find their solution. Critical idealism brings about an understanding of the same events as, on the one hand, those effected by nature's mechanism and, on the other, those traceable to a free intelligible ground, by proving the ideality of space and time and thus providing an insight into the nature of the causality of the phenomenal world. Hence it may be combined with the scientific justification of the presupposition of our moral judgment in so far as the latter also endeavors to sever an act from nature's mechanism. Our actions are phenomena, and solely as phenomena do they stand in connection with the mechanism of nature. As phenomena, they permit themselves, therefore, to be dissociated from the mechanism of nature and, being traced back to our "intelligible self," understood as free. As a result of the combination with critical idealism, the problem of freedom has assumed also the presuppositions of the methods of investigation of critical idealism. In the formulation urged upon us by our consciousness of moral responsibility, the problem of freedom has been reduced to a form which exhibits advantages on all counts over the method of investigation of critical idealism.

In posing the problem of freedom, the moral subject starts with himself: How can I present every one of my actions as free to myself in order not to be obliged to understand the moral law which expresses itself in my conscience as an illusion? Not until the question has been answered does the subject pass on to the analogous mode of judging with reference to other subjects. In this manner, the posing of the problem of freedom in its most natural form harbors the main presuppositions of the method which critical idealism uses in its investigations (provided critical idealism wishes to establish contact with the realm of the practical use of reason)—in other words, the identity of the knowing and the acting subject and the isolation of action with reference to the subject in so far as only thus the double mode of looking at the act as intelligible and as phenomenon suggests itself as a matter of course. For, as soon as the subject externalizes itself, the identification of act and appearance is no longer possible, since there exist only appearances then, but no longer any acts. Should one, nevertheless, wish to apply this designation, with all its consequences, to a series of phenomena, this can only happen on the basis of a conclusion arrived at by analogy, which deems itself justified in reducing a series of appearances to an intelligible subject and, of necessity, understanding that intelligible subject also as a unity of a knowing and an acting subject. The moral law urges us to take this step because it has reference to the mutual relationships between moral beings and has no meaning apart from the presupposition of a plurality of moral beings. The moral law can be satisfied with the conclusion by analogy, in asserting the existence of other moral beings apart from the subject which experiences the moral law in himself, a conclusion in which a number of appearances are referred, as acts, to an intelligible, moral subject. Critical idealism is meant to be the foundation for this method, although in this point it is flatly opposed to such a procedure, since in general it allows for only one subject, the knowing subject, the "intelligible self," apart from which—or better, for which—there are only phenomena. The problem as to a plurality of knowing subjects does not occur to it at all; for the knowing subject (whatever it might be) which, in going through the thought processes of critical idealism, understands all events as phenomena, is for itself "the knowing subject" in regard to which there is only one world of phenomena and by which appearances are comprehended solely as acts if it comprehends itself as an acting subject. The moral and practical reason which is united with this intelligible subject as a knowing subject necessarily urges on to the establishment of a plurality of intelligible subjects in respect to which certain areas of phenomena are to be understood as acts. At the same time, however, with these acting subjects it establishes knowing subjects in that it has to present these subjects in analogy to its own intelligible self, which it understands as a unity of a knowing and an acting self. However, when this is accomplished the idealistic and critical presuppositions are dissolved.

Thus, a profound antagonism becomes noticeable when the method of investigation of critical idealism is conjoined with the tendencies of practical and moral reason. This antagonism, however mighty it is, slumbers so long as the practical, moral problems present themselves in a form commensurate with the methods of investigation used by critical idealism. This is the case, as was stated above, with the problem of freedom, so long as it regards the act in its relation to nature's mechanism and presents it as free for the purpose of moral self-judgment. This is the form in which it makes its first appearance in moral reflection. It unconsciously contains the presuppositions which allow the method of investigation used by critical idealism to be applied to itself.

It is in this manner, then, that the solution of the problem of freedom develops within the framework of critical idealism. In the grave struggle to lay the foundation for the possibility of a moral *Weltanschauung* with respect to the problem of freedom which we experience with Kant, critical idealism truly does what is expected of it. It offers the possibility of comprehending human actions—in so far as they present themselves to the knowing subject in their twofold nature as either appearances or intelligible actions —as acts of the subject which are free moral judgments.

The struggle now seems at an end, the problem of freedom settled safely. With profound moral earnestness, Kant, with a view to moral judgment, ventures to apply the scientifically acquired presupposition for freedom to a case in which the moral judgment could charge itself with harshness and injustice if the assumption of freedom were not scientifically backed. At that very moment, however, he pulls from under the formulation of the problem of freedom the presuppositions with which it had operated unconsciously thus far. With one stroke, it changes its complexion; the goal already in sight flees far off, and the path trod thus far ends at a gaping precipice in whose abyss the problem of freedom perceives its true image. Frightened, it steps back. Moving once again in the realm of critical idealism, it regains its former appearance while the true image of itself which it saw appears as a frightening dream.

We have now reached the full height of the problem. Yet let us glance at the foothills, above which the pinnacle we have reached is hardly visible to the observer in the plains, before we take a look into the abyss facing us. In what has already been stated, we asked the question whether or not Kant was conscious of the deep significance of the problem formulated in the *Critique of Practical Reason* (p. 121) where he touches upon the higher levels of the problem of freedom for reasons already noted. We gave the answer above by pointing out that the main problem appears only as a special case of the first formulation of the problem in the schematism of critical idealistic thinking, where the identity of the acting and judging subject forms the hidden presupposition throughout the discussion. It presents itself as the application of the moral judgment to the deeds of "born evildoers." Kant came to the conclusion "that the natural nexus of their deeds does not render necessary the evil nature of their wills, but, rather, that it is the result of freely accepted evil and unchangeable principles which make it all the more punishable."

The advance in the level of problems in *Religion Within the Limits of Reason Alone* (p. 19-20) consists in that this view is not activated one-sidedly to account for the evilness of nature, but is also extended to the assumption of the goodness of nature. Not until this double formulation was the problem fully recognized; and all other points in which the development of *Religion Within the Limits of Reason Alone* goes beyond the *Critique of Practical Reason* (p. 121) are only a natural consequence of the two-sided problem that we now have. The act of freedom on p. 121 of the

*Critique of Practical Reason* from which the nature of disposition is derived, signifies only a greater emphasis on the responsibility of practical behavior, which was established elsewhere already. Contrary to this, pp. 19 and 20 of *Religion Within the Limits of Reason Alone* demonstrate the two-sided problem—that it is really this unfathomable act of freedom which furnishes the basis of the responsibility for our actions. On p. 121 of the *Critique of Practical Reason* the once-assumed-evil maxims are represented as unchangeable and necessarily sensitive to progress, that is, progress toward evil. This view will, likewise, have to be dispensed with as provisional when the two-sided problem confronts us, unless we are to carry absurdity into the problem itself.

Now comes the third and most important step forward. In the episodic form of the problems in the *Critique of Practical Reason* (p. 121) it might appear acceptable that there is a mean between the bad and the good nature of the disposition. In this case, the evil nature of the will would have to be understood as an exception to the average nature of the will inclined toward evil. When the two-sided problem confronts us, this view falls by the wayside: There is no mean between the good and evil nature of the disposition. With this assertion (whose scope one fathoms correctly only when one is mindful that the assumption of an evil and a good maxim as a free act must always again be reduced to a maxim) Kant has arrived at a point at which the genius must of necessity take up the fight with the historically legitimated views. From this standpoint he then hurls his death-dealing missiles against everything within reach: the dogmatic theory of original sin, moral empiricism, as well as the ethical-psychological illusions from Seneca to Rousseau. One opponent above all had to be brought low: the person who robbed moral reflection of its dead seriousness and replaced it with his sickly over-stimulation in which the two extremes, moral indifference and moral exaggeration, could occur equally at will.

Good and evil form absolute contrasts. The actions which rise from the good or evil nature of the disposition must rest upon a free act in order to fall under moral responsi-bility. Therefore, the moral nature of the disposition itself must be reduced to an act of the subject. The act would not be free if it were based on the existence or nonexistence of sensibility. In rejecting this assumption, as in all other matters, the conclusions from the demands of freedom and the determination of good and evil as opposites, coincide. In this case, this leads to the necessary assumption that the good and evil nature of the disposition rests on the assump-tion of a maxim.

With this conclusion we have arrived at the limits of our insight. The difficulties now opening up consist in the following. 1) We are continually tempted to apply time perceptions to the act thought last when we trace back the assumption of the maxims, misled by the analogy which urges itself upon us with the causal series in the phenom-enal world. 2) In spite of the above insight or, rather, perhaps just because of the fact that owing to it the assump-tion of an influence of the sensibility on the coming about of the moral disposition is being rejected, the evilness as it occurs, just like the goodness as it appears, becomes com-pletely incomprehensible. 3) In that we go back to the factor of the origination of the rational being for the explanation of the above state of affairs—a reflection which we were completely relieved of in Kant's explanation of the field of investigation in critical idealism—we arrive at the conclusion that the moral condition of the disposition must be thought of as innate and yet may not be represented as such.

These are the main difficulties in the representation of the first origination of the nature of the moral disposition in general. If one keeps in mind Kant's conception of evil (unacceptance of the moral law as the only determining ground for one's maxims), he must add the verifiable fact that in so far as human experience goes, man is, in general, evil in his ethical disposition. But it is exactly with the consciousness of the moral law that, simultaneously, the type of evil disposition is given (which can be noted empirically in man's actions) if one remembers that man, according to Kant, cannot be good and evil at one and the same time. It is implied in the consciousness of responsibility that both motivations coexist in man, who is empirically evil. The following remains as the only possible solution: Evil consists in the form of subordination of the motivations!

Evil is radical in so far as it spoils the ground of all maxims. The consequences of this character of the natural evil inclination are the following: 1) The original *Anlage* toward the good within us consists in the fact that the sensuous drives are, in view of the origin of evil, not only not indifferent but that they may be designated as a natural inclination toward the good in so far as they are the presuppositions of a societal association in which the moral law is to unfold itself. Hence, regaining the original *Anlage* toward the good cannot consist in the acquisition of a lost motivation to do good, but only in purifying it, being the uppermost ground of all of our maxims. 2) The same difficulties as for the general two-sided mode of consideration discussed above appear when we wish to form a mental picture of the act imagined as possible of an assumption of a morally good disposition by reversing the relationship in the usual subordination of maxims. Only the difficulties turn out to be practically soluble here in so far as this timeless act presents itself to man as a development. (This was not possible when we reversed the relationships of the maxim from which follows the radically evil, since the process had to be transported into the condition of our existence as rational beings where it had not yet become conscious.) The timeless intelligible comprehension of this act, which was an insoluble necessity for the occurrence of the radically evil in order to hold on to the responsibility for our actions, loses its cogency when we try to present to ourselves the re-entry of the good principle. Why? Because while he is continually experiencing progress and reflecting on his moral accountability, the rational being does not need to experience within himself that unitary intuition divorced from time and space, but, rather, can leave it to that being for whom "this infinity of progress represents a unity," and to whom this change presents itself as revolution (p. 50).

It becomes perfectly clear in the discussion just concluded that we are in a different field of investigation from that of the *Critique of Pure Reason* and the *Critique of Practical Reason*. In the case of the *Critiques*, the possibility of a moral evaluation of every action was gained by virtue of the fact that each presented itself as an intelligible act, divorced from its space-time determination, to which space-time causality could not be applied. This unity of sensuous world and intelligible world took place under the more or less conscious presupposition of an identity of the acting and judging subject. In the present case, however, where we are dealing with the problem of *Religion Within the Limits of Reason Alone*, we can no longer avail ourselves of the possibility of such a solution. We may roughly formulate as follows the question as to the problem of freedom and moral responsibility in its profoundest form, and we do so with a view to the possibility of man to better himself as laid down in the discussion on p. 50. How can we hold on to the moral responsibility for human actions if the transition from the radically evil to the radically good is presented merely as a character development by stages while, in essence, it consists in a timeless act, and is thus incapable of being carried out in our imagination as rational beings? In these circumstances there is no longer any solution on the basis of the unity of man as an intelligible and a phenomenal being; that is, the solution has become impossible by virtue of the type of reflection in critical idealism. In order to maintain the requirement, the solution of the difference must be sought in the imagined evaluation of a being who represents himself as a postulate, which, according to the *Critique of Pure Reason* and the *Critique of Practical Reason*, is possible only on the ground of representing to oneself the possibility of freedom in an insight which critical idealism imparts! Here, on p. 50—where the problem of freedom in its most profound form lies in the shape of a quest after the possibility of changing one's disposition— it is demonstrated, in the juxtaposition of divine and human types of reflection, that the basic question is no longer soluble in the realm of critical idealism as a principle of investigation, because critical idealism is committed to seeking the solution in the juxtaposition of man as an intelligible and a phenomenal being! The difficulty which can no longer be solved here consists in the transference of the idea of development (made necessary by the higher problem of freedom) to the intelligible realm. . . .

The fact that we are involved in the methods of investigation of critical idealism—as is so evidently clear from pp. 128 and 129—is of decisive importance for what follows. Concerning its practical aspect, pure reason has the same need as in its theoretical aspect: to seek in all that is given that which is unconditioned, to comprehend everything in a unity. This unconditioned totality of the object of pure practical reason is comprehended under the name of "the highest good." To arrive at the highest apex of human understanding is a matter of establishing the unity of the total content of our empirical will with the moral law and its demands. However, in pursuance of the investigations of p. 133 ("Concerning the Dialectics of Pure Reason in the Determination of the Concept of the Highest Good") the fact appears that—if we believe we have solved the entire problem of freedom with the methods of investigation of critical idealism—we are completely under the spell of this method of investigation. Beginning at this point, the entire discussion concerning the highest good appears, henceforth, under the presuppositions of the method of investigation of critical idealism.

Up to now, this method of investigation only served to prove that for me as a rational being, and considering all my actions, intelligible freedom and necessary condition are to be thought of as compatible by virtue of the absolute demands of the moral law. From now on, the bringing about of the unity between the moral law and the world in general is carried on under the same special reflection. Thus, the general concept of the highest good is placed in relationship to the individual person, something that was not contained in the original nature of this concept. Here, in the last analysis, lies the cause of all the inconsistencies, mistakes, and inaccuracies which have been levelled against Kant's philosophy of religion, especially in this respect. Therefore, it is odd that all these alleged mistakes in regard to critical idealism are no mistakes at all since they rest merely on the strictly maintained presuppositions of its method of investigation. What, at first sight, one may attempt to explain as an incomprehensible change in the trend of Kant's thought thus appears inevitable. The unity of moral law and world in the highest good which, taken in a general sense, would lead to the demand for a world in which all changes take place according to the causality of the moral law, is necessarily interpreted as related to the individual rational being as a unity of virtue and happiness. That this in turn rests entirely on the isolation of the subject and the identity of the acting and evaluating person and results necessarily from it is clear from the whole presentation on p. 133. Classically formulated, we find the presupposition for this reflection in the following statement: "To stand in need of happiness, to be worthy of it, but, nevertheless, not to partake of it, cannot be reconciled at all with the perfect will of a rational being who is at the same time all-powerful, even though we are just experimenting with such a thought" (p. 133).

"Virtue and happiness together constitute the possession of the highest good in a person." On this basis, Kant now builds further. The connection of these two concepts is necessarily synthetic. The mode of combination may be expressed in this statement: "It is *a priori* (ethically) necessary to produce the greatest good through freedom of the will." "If, therefore, the greatest good is impossible according to practical rules, then also the moral law which demands that it be promoted must be illusory and, to a large extent, false because it is based on empty imaginary purposes." Ordinarily the reader discovers in this sentence of Kant's an exaggerated and illogical assertion. However, it would be more appropriate to look for the illogicality in the judgment of those who are completely in agreement with the presuppositions of the method applied and yet find it objectionable if Kant draws the correct inference. Incorporating happiness into the concept of the greatest good and offering this alternative are the natural consequences of the presuppositions of the method of investigation applied. Nevertheless, everybody feels that in the course of the investigations and between the indubitable assertion of the fact of the moral law and the formulation of the antinomy on p. 137 (which winds up with the objectionable assertion which makes the admitted fact shaky) there must have crept in a logical error which is responsible for the entire formulation of the antinomy.

Concerning the moral person, in so far as it may be determined in his nature by the pre-existence of his self, Kant has stated quite correctly in the first section of *Religion Within the Limits of Reason Alone* that we cannot in any possible statements concerning it go beyond what is given in the phenomenal world, that is, birth, however inexplicable the fact of the lapse into the "radically evil" and particularly our consciousness of responsibility remain in the face of it. If we do not include in the assumption of a continued existence the continuation of the moral person at all, then the above-cited Kantian assertion is based on a change in subject which is covered up by the double meaning of the word, person. Hence, we are also forced to give to the term, person, a coinage strange to the field of investigation of critical idealism. At the same time, the infrastructure which the *Critique of Pure Reason* builds up with respect to asserting the continuation of our self, is not able at all to support the structure reared on it.

These difficulties, which necessarily arise in the imperceptible movement toward a field of investigation foreign to the essence of critical idealism, consist in the fact that in the postulate of immortality the higher, unsolved problem of freedom dominates the development of thought in the manner described above. Now, the question is whether these same difficulties also narrow down the second postulate. From the outset, this seems quite natural since this second postulate, likewise, is reared on the formulation of the concept of the greatest good which is possible only in the apparent solution of the problem of freedom in general. Scrutinized in greater detail, this second postulate of the existence of "God" was already necessary for the assumption of the first one. If holiness consists in the complete appropriateness of the disposition to the moral law—and this condition is thinkable in the intelligence of a sensuous being only as an infinite development—then there is holiness concerning the moral disposition only when there is an intelligence in which we may presuppose such a development as a unitary, timeless act. The necessity of a postulate thus formulated, whose elements may be found in the solution of the antinomy as well as in the *Critique of Practical Reason* (pp. 148 and 149), cannot be dismissed if we are seriously concerned with the Kantian juxtaposition of good and evil in which every condition of the disposition must be thought of as being reducible to an intelligible act.

Kant's train of thought takes a different turn. There must exist a guarantee of the proportionality of virtue and happiness, since otherwise the requirement of furthering the greatest good would falter and the moral law would become illusory. It is on this requirement that the postulate is built. And we have to state again that establishing the postulate in this form is possible only if one leaves the field of investigation of critical idealism. This relocation has only become possible through the apparently solved problem of freedom. Only in this way could a free rational being be equated with the empirical rational being and the proportionality of virtue and happiness in the empirical world be suggested by formulating the concept of the highest good for the rational being. On this is later based the demand for "a cause in the totality of nature different from nature which contains the reason for this connection . . . between happiness and morality" (p. 150). In this connection two different natural causalities having objective validity are cited which, being so contradictory, cannot be justified at all on the basis of critical idealism. It is characteristic that Kant (on pp. 173 and 174) feels compelled to make excuses for this method in that he acknowledges the unjustifiability on the basis of the results of critical idealism: "I have stated above that in the world happiness (which is exactly proportional to moral worth) is not to be expected according to the course of nature alone, and may be deemed impossible, and that, therefore, the possibility of the highest good in this respect can only be admitted under the presupposition of a moral author of the world. I cautiously did not mention the limitation of this judgment to the subjective conditions of our reason in order not to make use of it until the manner of its verification could be determined more closely. In fact, the impossibility mentioned is merely subjective." The object of Kant's excuse is to show that he has concluded from this objectified subjective impossibility to a demand from which not the objective speculative positing of a God, but only the subjective and practical assumption of his existence, would flow. This explanation, however, does not go to the core of the method, since the question concerns not whether the thus posited postulated being is subjective or objective, but whether or not—if the fact of the moral law is not to become illusory—the requirement of proportionality of virtue and happiness in the sensuous world must lead, of necessity, to the additional postulate of a being who comprehends the two causalities into a higher unity, himself being the primary cause of the world. (In all this one should, of course, keep in mind that the juxtaposition of two causalities is founded merely in our subjective view.) The answer on the basis of critical idealism is, of course, only a No, since the mechanism of nature and intelligible causality are represented as different merely in our reason, so that the former is the sensuous appearance of the latter. In order to bring about this unity, the rational being does not ever need to assert an infinite being who differs from a natural cause. To assume one actually contradicts critical idealism.

For the moment it is sufficient to note in the interesting remark on pp. 173 and 174 the following: Kant in this one case admits that the infrastructure of establishing a postulate extends beyond the boundary posts of critical idealism, a fact of which we became aware when a recoinage could be noted in the terms with reference to the first postulate. Furthermore, the demand to further the highest good in this world is basic to establishing the second postulate. The contradictions with which we are concerned in dealing with the possibility of the highest good refer to the juxtaposition of a "realm of nature" and a "realm of morals" (p. 174). The latter distinction does not completely coincide with the juxtaposition of an intelligible and a phenomenal world which is common in critical idealism. The dull identification of the two, which becomes necessary as soon as the postulate of the existence of God takes rise (presumably on the basis of critical idealism), is presupposed when the postulate was established on pp. 149 and 150 ff. and then carried out. The necessary consequence of a juxtaposition of a natural mechanism and an intelligible causality justified merely subjectively in the realm of the investigation of critical idealism, was suddenly regarded as objectively real. This identification of the realm of morals with the intelligible world in itself signifies, in regard to the establishment of the second postulate, what the identification of the personality as an enduring unity in the fluctuations of phenomena was meant to convey in regard to the basis of the second postulate.

Thus, it has been demonstrated for the basic method regarding establishing the second postulate that central to it is the same operation as in the first postulate, that is, identification of a moral magnitude with an intelligible one. This identification cannot be made in critical idealism, however natural it may be in the ordinary view. In the case of the concept of the moral person, we have demonstrated this by showing how the determination of an orderly and steadily progressive development—that is, change—clings to this concept by virtue of its empirical determination. The same now also holds true for the moral world, the realm of ethics. It is already contained in the demand that although the realm of morals cannot be realized until infinity is reached, empirical rational beings should work on it. The realm of morals is the magnification of the moral person. The uppermost moral rational being, God, is the immortal soul magnified as a continuation to perfection of the moral person. In establishing the second postulate there is a large-scale repetition of what we have already experienced in the establishment of the first postulate. Just as in the first postulate the second one was already implied, so the first one is again carried over in a different form in the second one, as if it had not been solved yet.

Now it must be demonstrated that the establishment of the second postulate may be investigated critically according to the same points of view as the first one. First of all, it must appear surprising that the starting point of the second postulate is not at all based on the solution of the first one, despite the fact that it is preceded by the establishment of the first one. It is even identical with it, but is not based on the first one at all. Rather, in the course of the investigation, it again posits the first one covertly, and assumes it. This fact does not come to the fore at all in some of the presentations of Kant's philosophy of religion. The blame lies on the introduction of the investigation of the second postulate where, it is true, reference is made to the solution of the first one as if the second one did require the solution of the first one as a condition (p. 149). However, if there really were a connection between the two, the introduction would necessarily stand on the following reflection —that the highest good consists in the proportionality of virtue and happiness. If, however, happiness is the highest comparison thinkable of every absolutely perfect satisfaction possible, then only the highest moral perfection, that is, holiness, can correspond to it in the realm of morality.

Now, we have shown that holiness can be thought of as being realizable only in infinity, a fact on which the demand for the immortality of soul is based. Hence, in what follows, the postulate of the proportionality of happiness and morality should be justifiable only in this formulation: The fact of the moral law in us which lays down a synthetic combination of virtue and happiness in the concept of the highest good demands that to the holiness of the immortal soul, which has been presented by the above postulate as possible (not as necessary, it is to be noted), the happiness of this immortal soul should necessarily correspond. If the second postulate is not based on the first one by such reasoning, then it is not based on it at all, does not presuppose it in any sense whatsoever, and may turn out to be merely a parallel presentation of the development of the first postulate if, in the end result, the first postulate is presupposed. This assertion is quite to the point if we can show that, presupposing the above reflection, the second postulate is completely impossible. Also, on the basis of the requirement that holiness of the soul must correspond to happiness, no postulate whatever can be based which assumes a being who in himself unites the two mutually contrasting causalities asserted here, since both magnitudes included in the postulate are given in the intelligible world. Indeed, on the postulate of immortality, a second postulate —that of the existence of a highest moral being—can be established just as little as the assumption of a God of the nature described makes certain and real the necessary assumption of the possibility of the immortal soul's holiness. On p. 148, it is shown that the assumption of this highest being is necessary if we are to predicate the holiness of anything at all, since it is in his intelligence alone that infinite moral development presents itself as a condition— as holiness.

This impossibility we can trace back to its first foundations. The establishment of the first postulate has become necessary by virtue of the fact that by laying down the impossibility of holiness in place of the fictional free rational being (concerning which the concept of the highest good was developed in consequence of the problem of freedom, which was solved only apparently) suddenly the empirical rational being appears whom, on the basis of critical idealism, it is possible to prove free. In order to maintain the assertions made regarding the fictionally free rational being, this free rational being is projected into infinity as an immortal soul, possibly already possessing holiness, and conjoined into a unity with the empirical moral rational being by assuming an infinite moral development. Here lies the significance of the postulate of immortality as developed. Now we have, as a matter of fact, incorporated the old fictional free rational being as a subject into all of our assertions, whereby the possibility—or better, the necessity—of establishing postulates is rendered nugatory, and we have moved, once again, back into the position which preceded ascertaining the actual impossibility of holiness for the rational being in the sensuous world. The error uncovered there is again nullified. What has been denied the fictional subject by this assertion, whereby it became the empirical rational being, has been assured it again in another way by the assumption of an infinite possibility of development in its progress towards holiness. And now we have, once more, the subject to which the determination of the concept of the highest good has reference, that is, a free rational being in so far as there is no obstacle to the present or future adequate commensurability of its will with the moral law. The identity of this rational being is thus guaranteed in both cases in that the divine reason seizes upon the infinite progress toward holiness as holiness as an existing act.

Should what follows be incapable of being joined, in the reflection formulated above, with the solution given by assuming the postulate of immortality, then, in actuality, the empirically unfree rational being is posited again as the subject of assertions which were made concerning the free fictional rational being. The postulate developed upon this inconcealable contradiction is merely the repetition of the solution already given but left out of account. Thus, we are, on p. 149, on the same spot as on p. 146. Previously, the example was geared to the concept of virtue as something commensurate with the disposition toward a moral law, while now the example is geared to the concept of happiness. One might just as well have begun with the latter example—in which case one would have also solved the former by implication. For the two concepts of morality and happiness stand in a relation of proportionality to each other, whereby the changes in magnitude must correspond with each other. The example is so construed that at one time a finite concept above is made to correspond with an infinite one below; the next time, the proportion is simply reversed. The solution consists in that through rendering infinite the finite side (the real essence of the postulate), equality is achieved on both sides.

Twice thus far we have made use of the general observations on pp. 158 to 177 and found both times that Kant definitely returns to the position of critical idealism which he occasionally left in establishing the second postulate. But now it turns out that all discussions in this context have the same tendency, that is, to demonstrate the true agreement of the results which the *Critique of Practical Reason* and the *Critique of Pure Reason* have achieved independently of each other. We already noted a similar suggestion after the problem of freedom had apparently been settled: "I may be permitted to call attention to only one more thing at this occasion; that is, that every step one makes with pure reason, even in the practical field, where one does not pay any notice at all to subtle speculation, nevertheless seeks contact, meticulously and involuntarily, with all the factors of the *Critique of Theoretical Reason*, as if each one had been thought through with premeditated caution, just to procure the necessary confirmation" (p. 128).

The postulates were, then, established without concern for the "ideas" of speculative reason in that immortality and the existence of God were arrived at solely by the demands of practical reason, as has been shown in the earlier section, "Concerning the Primacy of Pure Practical Reason in its Connection with the Speculative Reason." When the postulate of immortality was established, the reference that it corresponds to an idea of speculative reason was left out. With reference to the second postulate, it is pointed out nonchalantly on p. 151 that what is postulated here corresponds to a hypothesis of theoretical reason. The structure has now been erected; and in order to insert the capstone firmly, it is merely a matter of showing that through this independent procedure of practical reason only the ideas of theoretical reason have been legitimized. With this intention, the things to be remembered concerning the concept of God are enumerated (p. 166), and transcending the determination of critical idealism, when laying the groundwork for the second postulate, is referred to as unessential (p. 173).

Let us survey once more by way of review the road we have travelled in the investigations thus far before we pass on to a comparison of the results of practical reason and the way in which they are realized with the results of that section of the *Critique of Pure Reason* dealing with the philosophy of religion with which we have already concerned ourselves.

At first, we saw how freedom relative to the moral judgment of our actions was presented, on the basis of the antinomy of the moral law, as imperative and experienced in the fact of conscience in that a sharp distinction was made between it and every empirical motive force for action. The structure was built with the material of critical idealism. The practical idea of freedom was realized according to the scheme of a philosophy of religion in the transcendental dialectic. In consequence of the thus necessitated borrowing of the method of investigation in that scheme, the problem of freedom was looked upon as apparently fully solved; with respect to the free rational being, a demand was made for the highest good presented as a synthetic unity of virtue and happiness. This is the formulation of the demands for a moral world in general, which is imperative, considering the isolated person. Asserting the impossibility of holiness on the one hand, and of happiness on the other, the empirically unfree rational being returns to investigate further. The demand for freedom in the face of the moral law in which the demand for a moral world in general is equally posited (which is immediately clear if we start with the community of all moral rational beings) reappears in the demand for a highest good which, in turn, is again only the demand of the individual for a moral world and leads to the postulates of immortality and the existence of God. Since the solution of the problem of freedom is not possible on the higher levels of stating the problem in the field of investigation of critical idealism, the realm of critical idealism is transcended in all statements at whose base we somehow find this problem. We have proven this for the section on the radically evil. Likewise, we found that the postulates regarding the formulation and statements did not stay within the bounds of critical idealism. They are "postulates" but not ideas. Only one idea is realized, the idea of freedom. In order to reach the triad and the systematic connection by which they could legitimatize themselves as ideas (cf. *Critique of Pure Reason*, p. 385), the three magnitudes realized thus far quit the series and the connection in which they had stood up to now and in which they had been realized. They immediately adopt the sequence and systematic connection which the three ideas in the process of entering the practical field exhibited on p. 385 of the *Critique of Pure Reason*. This procedure, however, is possible because the two postulates are not ideas. At their base lies the higher problem of freedom, which is beyond critical idealism. We may, therefore, reduce the insight won in the tedious investigation thus far to a double expression based on one fact: 1) The problem of freedom as it presents itself in its profoundest formulation on the factual basis of the moral law is insoluble with the means at the command of critical idealism, or 2) the postulates of the existence of a highest moral rational being and the infinite continuation of person (immortality) realized as necessary within us by the practical use of reason based on the fact of the moral law within us, do not lie in the realm of critical idealism and, therefore, do not coincide with the ideas of a highest being and the timelessness of our intelligible existence, which critical idealism has demonstrated as problematic and religiously oriented.

Thus, we can note the curious fact that it is only on the basis of critical idealism that the ideas of God, freedom, and immortality have been established as possible without science being able to claim otherwise in the interest of truth, but that these ideas immediately undergo a transformation as soon as this possibility has been raised into a practically recognized reality by virtue of the experience of the moral law. The transformation is of such a nature that the scientific demonstration of its possibility can no longer be accomplished with the means at the command of critical idealism. The hope of realizing these problematic ideas through the fact of the moral law must, therefore, be given up according to the investigation of the sections of the *Critique of Pure Reason* and the *Critique of Practical Reason* in which the philosophy of religion is dealt with. The assertion on p. 591 of the *Critique of Pure Reason* has not materialized: "In what follows it will become evident, however, that respecting its practical use, reason has the right to assume something it is not authorized by any manner or means to presuppose without sufficient proof in the field of mere speculation."

This means nothing else but that the scheme of a philosophy of religion in the transcendental dialectic which was meant to prepare the way for the philosophy of religion of critical idealism was not thoroughly worked out. Up to now we have considered two attempts in detail which, in temporal sequence, were meant to carry out this scheme, and we found that the first of the two, the sketch of a philosophy of religion, does not yet know the scheme of the philosophy of religion in the transcendental dialectic, while the second one, the *Critique of Practical Reason,* knows it, to be sure, but is not able to execute it logically. Both times the question of in how far the completion of the scheme of the transcendental dialectic has succeeded concerns fixing the position which the idea of freedom during the realization of the ideas occupies vis-à-vis the two other ideas. Let us compare the two attempts briefly.

We have shown that on pp. 608 and 609 of the *Critique of Pure Reason* the practical idea of freedom is understood as if it were not a problem of reason in its practical interest, but merely a question of two problems: Is there a God; and is there a future life? By means of our investigation of the concepts of freedom which come into play in Kant's thinking in general, we have shown that no progress at all was made with the practical freedom thus understood, and that the existence of God and immortality of soul may not be deduced from the presupposed possibility of a moral world (p. 612). Both demands are made on the assumption, recognized as necessary, of the proportionality of virtue and happiness, which is to the same degree implied in the theoretical as in the practical use of reason. "Therefore I say that just as moral principles according to reason in its practical use are necessary, it is just as necessary, according to reason in its theoretical use, to assume that everyone has cause for expecting happiness to the same extent to which he makes himself worthy of it by his behavior; and that, therefore, the system of morality is inseparably connected with that of happiness, but only in the idea of pure reason" (p. 613). Now follows the realization of the two remaining ideas and, to be sure, in the reverse order from that in practical reason: first the idea of God; then the idea of immortality (p. 614). If we take proper note of the motivation, we find that both are based merely on the principle of happiness and the immortality of soul does not result from the demands for infinite moral perfection. Kant is so far removed from this thought that he prefers to presuppose a meritorious moral behavior in this world upon which the future world will follow. "Since of necessity we must, by virtue of reason, think ourselves as belonging to a moral and intelligible world—although the senses give us nothing but a world of appearances—we shall have to assume the moral and intelligible world as the result of our behavior in the sensuous world, but lying in the future, because the sensuous world does not offer us any immediate approach. Thus, God and a future life are two presuppositions not to be separated from the obligation which pure reason, according to its own principles, exacts" (p. 614).

We now also have the confirmation of the assertion made and demonstrated earlier that the realization of the postulates in practical reason may take place in a different sequence and without the distribution according to which the postulate of the existence of God builds upon the postulate of happiness and immortality on that of holiness as the second constituent of the highest good. For, with the one the other is always given, because both reflect (though in different ways) the requirements of the rational being to be placed in a world where the moral law is the principle of events. This difference in the arrangement in the sketch of a philosophy of religion and the *Critique of Practical Reason* lies in the fact that in the former the realized magnitudes are not yet ideas, and in the latter they are no longer ideas. The escalation which drives the realized magnitudes beyond the concept of ideas in the *Critique of Practical Reason* took place by a deepening of the ethical content.

Freedom is also realized as an idea in the *Critique of Practical Reason* as compared with the sketch of a philosophy of religion. What has been brushed aside in the *Critique of Pure Reason* almost as if it were just a preliminary remark (pp. 608 and 609: "Now, then, we should first take note of the fact that for the time being . . .") is again treated in the critical light of the analysis of pure practical reason (pp. 108 to 129 of the *Critique of Practical Reason*) in a discussion where every line once more reveals the mighty struggle of the spirit with the problem. What a difference between the manner in which the problem concerning transcendental freedom is shoved aside as of no concern on p. 608, where it is a question of the practical use of reason, and the confession with which Kant announces his victory in the *Critique of Practical Reason.* He says, on p. 124 of the *Critique of Practical Reason:* "Of such great importance is the separation of time as well as of space from the existence of things-in-themselves as I have accomplished it in the critique of pure speculative reason. However, the solution of the difficulty here expounded, some might say, is weighed down very heavily and is hardly susceptible to a clear exposition. Nevertheless, is every other attempt at solution which has been made and may yet be undertaken easier or more comprehensible . . .?" The resignation manifested in these words has something profoundly stirring about it if one has, by studying the text, experienced vitally with Kant the entire treatment of the problem of freedom in the *Critique of Practical Reason.*

Let us summarize briefly the result offered us by the investigation of the *Critique of Practical Reason* for an insight into Kant's philosophy of religion.

To be sure, the *Critique of Practical Reason* contains Kant's presentation, which is to represent the philosophy of religion of critical idealism. However, this is not the outline of a consistent thought structure of his philosophy of religion, because it carries out the scheme of a philosophy of religion in transcendental dialectics—which rests upon the unity of pure reason in theoretical and practical use—only half of the way, and then reproduces the original plan of the *Critique of Practical Reason* which, in essence, and by virtue of the dynamism residing in the moral law, as it is grasped more fully right along, transcends the bounds of critical idealism. The scheme of a philosophy of religion in transcendental dialectics was never realized in full by Kant. It would have led him into a philosophy of religion of "pure reason in practical use," while the *Critique of Practical Reason* has already offered us the philosophy of religion of "practical reason."

Thus, at the conclusion of our scrutiny of the *Critique of Practical Reason,* we find Kant's philosophy of religion in the process of moving steadily and necessarily toward a field which no longer lies within the bounds of critical idealism. This movement is most pronounced in the emergence of the higher problem of freedom in the *Critique of Practical Reason.* And, thus, we proceed to that piece of writing which we have already utilized in the treatment of our problem of freedom.

## Religion Within the Limits of Reason Alone

The first part of the essay *Concerning Radical Evil in Human Nature* is an exposition of the higher problem of freedom. In the first essay of *Religion Within the Limits of Reason Alone*, the problem of freedom is also basic. A certain dependence on the biblical and dogmatic use of language which obscures the clarity of exposition in this first piece is noticeable. If we survey the work as a whole, a new difficulty in the way of clarity in the development of thought raises its head—lying in the conception of this work and resting mainly on the independent nature of the first essay as compared with the others. Both difficulties together have as consequence that one does not immediately see clearly how the inner development of thought in *Religion Within the Limits* proceeds in complete analogy to that of the *Critique of Practical Reason*, but only that it presents itself as a repetition of the latter on the basis of the more profoundly grasped problem of freedom, whereby similarities and deviations appear almost at once. The questions as to the relationship of the *Critique of Practical Reason* and *Religion Within the Limits* is almost insoluble, should one presuppose the former in evaluating the latter.

We shall start with a comprehensive review of the first essay. Earlier we tried to show that the problem of freedom in its higher version lies at the basis. In view of the moral evaluation of human actions, how can we think of a possibility of one natural state of our disposition passing over to another one in so far as this is absolutely required for the maintenance of our freedom to act? The impossibility of a solution is further increased by Kant's version of an absolute contradiction between good and evil in so far as the occurrence of the good or evil nature of the disposition —in respect to necessity and point of time—lies as an intelligible act beyond human understanding, and we can think of a change in the moral sense only as a constant progress. The task of the first section consists in the presentation of the entire profundity of the problem as is already indicated in the title, "Concerning the Indwelling of the Evil Principle Beside the Good One."

In the interest of moral stamina, Kant offers a summary solution to the problem by asserting that the intelligence of God comprehends moral development—thought of as infinite—into a unitary act according to which "change" may be considered "as revolution" in the moral judgment of God. At this point both difficulties work together, that is, the one founded in the conception of the work itself, as well as the one brought about by reliance on the religious, biblical, and dogmatic views. The result is that the further pursuit of this thought is not permitted to come clearly to the light of day. To say it plainly, Kant overlooks the lack of justification for introducing the concept of God at this point. The problem of the possibility of the fall and resurrection exists for the moral self-evaluation of man, not for the imagined evaluation of God, whose existence must first be proven to rest upon the practical demand of the moral law. Thus, we are dealing here with an accompanying realization of the idea of God as we had already occasion to note when Kant established the postulate of immortality in the *Critique of Practical Reason*. In general, it may be said that the last-mentioned passage has great affinity with the one at hand and rests upon the same procedure.

It may still be fresh in our memory how establishing the existence of God in the *Critique of Practical Reason* went hand in hand with the practical assumption of immortality and how, in the postulate of the existence of God as guarantor of the intelligible moral world, immortality was established right along with it, in so far as it is thought of as participation in that world. The same is the case with *Religion Within the Limits of Reason Alone*, when the first difficulty is dissolved. It is brought about in that we think of the total moral evaluation of our existence as taking place in the absolute intelligence of the highest moral being. In this way, the existence of this being is practically demonstrated as real. At the same time, however, our supersensuous existence is established right along with this as the imagined continuation of our earthly existence in so far as we are meant to receive the reward for our conduct in the judgment of the highest moral being. This section of *Religion Within the Limits of Reason Alone* also arrives at

the practical assumption of the continuation of our existence; but this result is radically different from the practical
assumption of immortality in the *Critique of Practical
Reason*. The two trains of thought have absolutely nothing
in common and move in different directions at every point.
In the *Critique of Practical Reason* immortality is postulated in the interest of the infinite moral development. In
*Religion Within the Limits of Reason Alone*, this development is thought of as finished with life on earth, and
positing a future life which takes no interest whatever in
moral development offers difficulties, particularly because
of the fact that it prolongs the moral contradictions into
eternity and thus renders an intelligible moral world impossible—the very thing for which the *Critique of Practical
Reason* established immortality as a postulate! Now we
become aware that the identification of the intelligible
substratum of the rational being and the moral personality
is incompatible with maintaining the moral evaluation of
our existence on earth and that it can be brought in harmony with it only if and when we can justify assuming
the most thoroughgoing dualism. The latter assumption,
however, contradicts the requirement of the realization of
the highest good thought of as a moral, intelligible world.
Thus also the moral law becomes illusory and the whole
investigation returns to nothingness.

In analyzing the first section in *Religion Within the
Limits of Reason Alone* one becomes aware of all these
difficulties without being able to fathom their scope fully;
the dogmatic use of language covers up the complete other-
ness which lies in the expressions "immortality" and "a
future life" concerning their relationship to the infinite

moral development required by the moral law.

That advancing and developing the thought of the continuation of our existence exhibits a deep cleavage between the sketch of a philosophy of religion and the trend of thought of the *Critique of Practical Reason,* has already been shown. Now we have found that regarding this problem *Religion Within the Limits of Reason Alone* is closer to the *Critique of Pure Reason* and the *Critique of Practical Reason* in that both speak of a future life and do not motivate this idea with the necessary assumption of an infinite moral development of our personality. This assumption constitutes the basis for establishing the postulate of immortality in the *Critique of Practical Reason* which is apparently realized in the identification of the moral person with the intelligible substratum of the rational being on the basis of critical idealism. The comprehensive moral evaluation of our existence on earth is of no interest in this reflection, especially on account of the continuity of the moral development which brings our earthly existence together with intelligible existence in the concept of the postulate of immortality. Intelligible existence is unhesitatingly equated with existence in the moral world by the identification of the latter with the intelligible world. Contrary to this in the sketch of a philosophy of religion and in *Religion Within the Limits of Reason Alone* there reposes, on the threshold between this world and the next, a moral judgment which strikes the balance of our behavior in the sensuous world. The sketch of a philosophy of religion expresses it in this manner on p. 614: " . . . we have to look at the moral world as a consequence of our behavior in the sensuous world." On the same page, however, the identification of the moral world with the intelligible one wants to be kept. But in doing so, the interpretation of the future world as a consequence of our moral behavior in the world of sense has become illusory because the presupposed moral judgment of our behavior on earth has to maintain the possibility of a double ending—in which case future existence cannot be equated with life in the moral world. Thus, the sketch of a philosophy of religion occupies a position midway between the *Critique of Practical Reason* and *Religion Within the Limits of Reason Alone*. With the latter it shares the concept of a "future life" and the relationship between the continuation of our existence and the moral evaluation of our behavior on earth. With the former it shares the identification of the moral world with the intelligible one, a difficulty which makes itself noticeable in the use of the indefinite articles when the concept of the intelligible world is introduced. Thus, the sketch of a philosophy of religion encompasses a contradiction regarding the continuation of our existence relative to the moral evaluation of our earthly life, a contradiction which the deeper probing of the problem in the *Critique of Practical Reason* and *Religion Within the Limits of Reason Alone* brings right out into the open. The two reflections are joined together in the sketch of a philosophy of religion because the practical assumption of a highest good, of a moral world ruler, and of the highest derived good precede the moral world, the positing of a future life. At the same time, it has been established that the concept of God as a moral lawgiver and judge was introduced into the investigation prior to the assumption of a future existence, and, thus, the personality is being developed which can evaluate its existence in a future moral world as the consequence of its behavior in this sensuous world. It is characteristic that in the reflection which derives a future existence from a moral pronouncement of God as judge of the moral behavior in this world and which arrives at the concept of God as moral creator of the world and lawgiver, there must precede the introduction of a demand for the infinite continuation of our existence. In the *Critique of Practical Reason,* where the moral judgment concerning our terrestrial existence has no connection whatever with the postulate of immortality, the postulate of immortality is consistently disposed of prior to the postulate of the existence of God as a moral creator of the world and lawgiver. *Religion Within the Limits of Reason Alone* is in a similar position; a future existence is implied in assuming a moral judgment of our existence by God's intelligence. The relocation of moral judgment into God's infinite intelligence is the only possibility of solving the difficulty, which consists in the fact "that the distance between the good we ought to do and the bad with which we start is infinite and, in so far as the act is concerned (that is, the commensurability of a way of life with the holiness of the law), is not attainable at any time."

Now, with the fact of the moral law, first of all my own personality is given as the subject of moral evaluation. If the moral evaluation is to be transferred into God's infinite intelligence because of the difficulties which result from defining good and evil as absolutely contradictory concepts, then it is absolutely necessary that in a preliminary discussion the concept of God as a moral lawgiver and moral judge be demonstrated as a practically necessary assumption. This, however, is not the case in the section of *Religion Within the Limits of Reason Alone* under consideration. The concept of God as moral creator of the world, lawgiver and judge is, to be sure, presupposed in so far as the entire presentation is made to depend upon Christian dogmatic thoughts and phrases. The real act of establishing this concept by moral deliberation does not occur until p. 101 ff., as we have shown at the beginning of this section. The connection between the concept of God and the moral law also met with in this section of *Religion Within the Limits of Reason Alone* is not to be supported by Kant's earlier writings, since the deliberation is entirely different in the *Critique of Practical Reason*, and the moral concept of God is arrived at only after the postulate of immortality. Thus, the foundation is lacking for solving the difficulties on p. 68 ff. By leaning on the dogmatic statements of Christianity, an apparent foundation is invented and the main moral difficulty of the Kantian philosophy of religion, that is, of the connection of the moral law with the concept of God, is apparently overcome. The basic intention of Kant's "philosophic doctrine of religion," to derive all statements made on the basis of the moral law and the practical requirements resulting therefrom, has been given up as a matter of fact.

These difficulties, which have been solved only by an unintentional deception, all go back to the one thought of the inappropriateness of the duration of our existence as a postulate for infinite moral development. They caught our attention by virtue of the fact that in the place of man in general, individual man as a subject entered Kant's thinking. At the moment when general considerations come to the fore again and man is introduced as the subject of investigation, especially on account of his standing in a societal relation with mankind, the difficulties disappear and the infinity of moral development is in consonance with the unimaginable duration of mankind in general. The investigation at the beginning of the third section of the philosophical doctrine of religion is on level ground. The phrasing of this title, "Concerning the Victory of the Good Principle over Evil," is meant to express the progress of thinking in this third section vis-à-vis the second section ("The Struggle of the Good Principle with Evil"). The question is now merely whether thought has progressed organically. If we keep in mind that in the second section it is a matter of man considered as an individual, and that man in general (in so far as he comprehends within himself the societal bond with mankind) is the subject under consideration and dominating the presentation in the third; and if, furthermore, one is aware of how little the third section refers back to the second one, one will rather incline toward the assumption that in both sections basically the same problem is treated under different presuppositions about the subject. The resolution of this problem depends on the investigation of the reflections in this third section.

Concerning our comparison, we have seen that the sketch of a philosophy of religion is much closer to the discussions of *Religion Within the Limits of Reason Alone* than the *Critique of Practical Reason*, because the former implies the thought of developing and expanding a moral community in its concept of the highest good, while it shares with the latter the formulation of the concept of happiness.

Thus, the sketch of a philosophy of religion occupies, in regard to all points adduced above whose consequences extend to every imaginable point of comparison, a transitional place between the *Critique of Practical Reason* and *Religion Within the Limits of Reason Alone*. This is particularly plain in the formulation of the concept of the kingdom of God in its relation to the development of the moral community of mankind and the concept of God derived from it. The sketch is aligned with the thought of the *Critique of Practical Reason* because in both, the practical moral investigation point, by formulating the concept of happiness beyond the boundaries of the world in which man is understood as a moral person and his action in general is placed in opposition to what is happening in the world. In that the endpoint of the moral development is relocated in the beyond, the value of the moral appraisal of the this-worldly moral development is weakened. This is shown in that neither the *Critique of Practical Reason* nor the *Critique of Pure Reason* occupies the standpoint at the end of their discussions from which the necessity, or, perhaps only possibility (cf. the *Critique of Practical Reason*), may be derived of taking up the ethical evaluation of the moral and societal institutions of mankind in regard to the final moral purpose which is envisaged as the highest good. *Religion Within the Limits of Reason Alone,* however, is forced, in spite of the difficulties facing it, to bring the ideal magnitudes into relationship with their empirical historical presentation and to bring the religion of reason into union with the pronouncements of historical religion. Although the latter is done at the expense of the perspicuity and independence of the reflections, incorporating this intention into the scheme of the presentation is quite characteristic. It is in line with the possibility of appreciating the political, civil community as a precondition for the ethical community. Now we have seen how, in the *Critique of Practical Reason*, when we were going beyond the present world (taking our stand on the fact of the moral law and looking toward the endpoint of ethical development), we were led to the absolute impossibility of appreciating human conditions ethically as soon as we tried to reverse the reasoning. In *Religion Within the Limits of Reason Alone* we meet the case that the emphasis in the presentation lies particularly on the possibility of bringing historical phenomena into relationship with the ideal magnitudes of moral deliberations. The question now is whether this presentation may, with attaining the final moral purpose in view, go consistently beyond the limits of the given world, as concerns the moral person in his individuality or in his wholeness.

This is not the case for the concept of the kingdom of God as a moral end which was reached under the general mode of reflection, as is already evident from the subtitle of the third section: "Concerning the Founding of a Kingdom of God on Earth." However, the second section, which deals with the individual moral person, goes beyond these limits in that it posits a future existence in which, as we are about to enter it, a divine judgment points to happiness or damnation. We have already shown above that the thus-understood supersensuous existence presents itself as a "future life," not as "immortality of soul," because it has no connection with the ethical development of personality regarding infinite perfectibility. This supersensuous existence has no moral interest. The above reflection still requires proof that the assertion of such a "future existence" cannot be established at all on the fact of the moral law, taking into consideration the presuppositionlessness demanded by the moral investigation.

The transfer of the final moral judgment into the intelligence of God—in so far as a future existence is implied in it—was executed in the second section only under the presupposition that the practical reality of the concept of God may be assumed as given and the connection of the same with the moral law as already accomplished. However, this was not actually the case, and the recognition that the moral concept of God is not actually reached until well along in the third section remained under cover by virtue of the confusion of the presentation with the religious-dogmatic pronouncements of historical Christianity. Thus, the motivation of the future existence introduced hypothetically into the second section crumbles of its own weight by recognizing the deceptive appearance of its basic presuppositions.

We now proceed to summarize briefly the ideas by which a place may be assigned to *Religion Within the Limits of Reason Alone* in the entire development of Kant's philosophy of religion. If one leaves the concealing cover out of account for the moment, we find that *Religion Within the Limits of Reason Alone* seizes upon three ideas as problems, and deals with them. In spite of the identical expression, we are not operating on the ground of critical idealism. For the ideas which are being discussed in *Religion Within the Limits of Reason Alone* have reference to the community of ethical beings and stand in connection with the clearly recognized main problem of freedom which is discussed in the first section. On this are then established the ideas of a perfected ethical personality, of a perfected moral community and the highest moral personality, that is, the moral lawgiver. Now, the first and second ideas form one whole because they can be brought to perfection only in a mutual relationship. The moral personality arises and becomes reality only in the ethical community. The question as to the possibility of the perfection of the ethical personality, however, coincides with the problem of freedom on the higher level of the problem. Thus, we have only two ideas in *Religion Within the Limits of Reason Alone*—the higher idea of freedom and the idea of God. The idea of immortality has dropped out because its ethical interest comes to the fore in the higher formulation of the problem of freedom. But also the idea of God in *Religion Within the Limits of Reason Alone* is only a subsidiary concept called in to make the "ethically common being" in whom the ethical personality is to perfect itself, comprehensible. In reality, *Religion Within the Limits of Reason Alone* knows only one idea, the idea of freedom in its higher formulation. The whole of Kant's philosophy of religion, complete in this form, oriented toward one question, is: How is the ethical personality of man as a moral creature regarding his essence and perfectibility possible in this world? In that *Religion Within the Limits of Reason Alone* is being guided by this questioning into stressing the ethical community, a modern trend wafts through these thoughts in spite of the dogmatic and churchy phraseology, a trend which is invigorating because of the great profundity of the moral consciousness which here struggles into form. The vitality of ethical thought has pushed thinking out of the narrow track in which critical idealism had coerced the Kantian philosophy of religion. Simultaneously, with the freedom of mobility, it garners in the full wealth of thought which it exhibited already in its undeveloped form before it was put in a consistent relationship to critical idealism. *Religion Within the Limits of Reason Alone* refers back to the sketch of a philosophy of religion, while it shows almost no contact with the *Critique of Practical Reason*. The *Critique of Practical Reason* represents a stage in the development of Kant's philosophy of religion. It is, as it were, a narrow pass through which Kant's mental army had to go on its march from the area of precritical rudimentary development to the area of complete maturity of thought. Thus, *Religion Within the Limits of Reason Alone* represents the highest perfection of Kant's philosophy of religion. Its thoughts are modern. In this treatise Kant stands far above his time in his thinking, if not in the language he used. This is shown also in that he is able to fuse the contradictory trends of the religious thinking of his time, rationalism and pietism, into a higher unity, as if they already belonged to the past, and he does so by fighting them in their one-sidedness from his higher position. If we have comprehended this innermost core of the thinking in *Religion Within the Limits of Reason Alone* in its entire depth, we must doubly bemoan the fact that Kant, forced by unfavorable circumstances, cloaked his up-to-date thoughts in the stiff dogmatic form of the church language of his day, perhaps more than was called for by his pedagogic wisdom; and thus, the depth of his thought became veiled almost to the present day, making it possible to look upon his profoundest work in the philosophy of religion as a retreat from the *Critique of Practical Reason* and, thus, to leave it out of account in the treatment of his philosophy of religion.

# The *Critique of Judgment*

⊐ It is hardly necessary after what has been said, and without concern over the chronology of Kant's writing, to justify our having treated *Religion Within the Limits of Reason Alone* prior to the *Critique of Judgment*. The detailed investigation of the solution to the problem of freedom led us to pursue further the development of a thought in *Religion Within the Limits of Reason Alone* left incomplete in the *Critique of Practical Reason*. Thus, also, it became necessary to compare the further development in thinking in both works which an interpolated treatment of other works would have made more difficult. The points of comparison of the *Critique of Judgment* concerning its thought on the philosophy of religion lie, to a large part, more toward the sketch of a philosophy of religion. The *Critique of Judgment* brings to a conclusion the thoughts of the series of ideas that stood foremost in the sketch of a philosophy of religion in that it furnishes a capstone to the introduction of the concept of "the final end of creation."

Thus, there also occur odd agreements with the thoughts in the sketch of a philosophy of religion in the treatment of the individual problems, while the *Critique of Practical Reason* moves closer to being included in the comparison not until the end of the *Critique of Judgment*, because of the unjustified introduction of the immortality concept and, at the same time, shifting the entire thinking away from its original aim.

We shall start with an investigation of the problem of freedom. The *Critique of Judgment* treats the problem as solved. It no longer occupies itself with it but goes back to earlier formulations in those passages where it touches upon the problem. In this way the dependence on the sketch of a philosophy of religion becomes more pronounced than in the *Critique of Practical Reason*. The main passage which is in question here may be found on p. 370 of the *Critique of Judgment*: "The idea of freedom is a fact whose reality, as a special kind of causality (whose concept, theoretically considered, would be an exaggeration), may be demonstrated in the practical laws of pure reason and, in accordance with these, in real actions, hence in experience. It is the only one among all ideas of pure reason whose object is a fact and which must also be reckoned among the *scibilia*."

Here is the idea which we can pursue into the details of terminology, on the basis of which in the *Critique of Pure Reason* (pp. 608 and 609) practical freedom was disposed of before the practical attainment of the two religiously oriented ideas. Again, the *Critique of Judgment* picks up once more the scheme of a philosophy of religion in transcendental dialectics and incorporates an exposition of it.

In this side-by-side arrangement of ideas which before had determined the entire presentation of a philosophy of religion, and in the offhand manner in which they are inserted into the *Critique of Judgment* in a subordinate place, is demonstrated that the *Critique of Judgment* occupies a far more developed position and carries fragments of a past exposition with it just as a river carries debris with it. The idea which touches upon the scheme of a philosophy of religion in transcendental dialectics stands in connection with the explanation in the *Critique of Pure Reason* (p. 591) before the play of transcendental hypotheses begins: "It will be shown in what follows that regarding its practical use, reason has the right to assume something which it would in no wise be authorized to presuppose without sufficient proofs in the field of mere speculation."

The basic idea is that what will later legitimize itself practically as "idea" in the moral conception of existence has already turned out to be a hypothesis on attempting to grasp scientifically the totality of the world and as such was in equilibrium, as is seen in the fencing match on pp. 591 to 595 of the *Critique of Pure Reason*. Adding a practical moral interest becomes decisive. It procures the right of domicile in the practical field to the ideas that were born in the speculative field, but were not domiciled there. "An advantage appears on the side of one who maintains something as a practically necessary presupposition (*melior est conditio possidentis*)." The *Critique of Practical Reason* had abandoned this thought entirely; along with the practical need for postulates it maintained their practical assumption without going for support to the preparatory work of unity-seeking theoretical reason. This is especially

· 93 ·

clear when the concept of God is arrived at whereby no attention is paid to the teleological sketches of theoretical reason in the *Critique of Practical Reason*. The individual magnitudes are arranged in series and the reader is supposed to conceptualize for himself how what follows is based on what precedes it. The schematism of the projected reflection and the rather odd poverty of "ideas" as compared with those of the *Critique of Pure Reason* thus become understandable. The *Critique of Judgment* again guides us into the old tracks. Practical reason procures reality for the ideas which begin to appear over the horizon in the field of theoretical reflection. This thought is developed concerning the concept of God.

Let us look back over the road travelled thus far. We started with the basic problem lying at the root of the projected work: why progress in thinking, which lies at the base of the entire planning of the work, comes so little to the fore in the presentation of esthetic judgment. It is due to the fact that the main question which constitutes the peculiarity of synthetic judgments and the *a priori* principles of the ability to judge, as compared with all other means of knowledge, is not put at the beginning of the investigation. All difficulties which we have traced relative to this assertion were reduced to this circumstance. They consisted mainly in the irregularly occurring and vague coinage of new concepts whereby we were compelled to determine more closely the basic subject of the statements after we had started with the investigation of the use of the concept of the supersensuous in relation to the intelligible, unconditioned, and infinite, as well as its position and connection with the world of experience. While we were presenting the matter, we implied that the main question—that is, in how far the esthetic comprehension of the world is a connecting link between appraising it by means of understanding and reasoning morally—was neither taken note of nor solved in the plan of the *Critique of Esthetic Judgment*. It is a critique of taste aimed at arriving at and presenting the concepts of the beautiful and sublime without reference to the generality of esthetic judgment of the entire world of appearance; and, therefore, it is also incapable, in principle, of showing the connection with the other faculties of knowledge regarding which, when investigated, no barriers were drawn as to the field in question. And yet, achieving this connection together with insight into its necessary nature lies in the consistency of Kant's thinking, taking the whole field of esthetic judgment into consideration. This is already evident in the fact that Kant—although without native artistic ability and without ever having come in closer contact with the performing arts—was driven, almost against his own will and merely through the logic of his own thinking, into the comprehensive investigation of the *Critique of Esthetic Judgment*. So mighty, however, was the logic of his thinking that Kant (although still caught up in the narrowing down of the esthetic investigation as if it had reference only to the beautiful and sublime) breaks down the barriers which still cling to the plan of the *Critique of Esthetic Judgment* in the conclusions he reached. Morcover, he pointed out a new path for esthetic investigations whose course, however, is visible only for a short distance. But the leg no longer has the ability to start on a new journey.

In these reflections, the task of the second part of our present investigation is delineated. It is a matter of high-lighting and tying together the passages where Kant's investigation points beyond the self-imposed limits (the presentation of the beautiful and the sublime) and estab-lishes reference to the essence of the esthetic grasp of the world in general, whereby the nature of the synthesis accom-plished by the esthetic judgment and the peculiarity of the basic *a priori* principles appear. At the same time is won the knowledge of the necessity and solubility of the diffi-culties just alluded to. In finding the reasons for the last of the difficulties which concern the fixation of the subject implied in the esthetic judgment, we grasp the nature of the fact and the innermost essence of the link which the esthetic judgment forges between our grasp of the world according to the understanding and according to moral reason as well.

If . . . an opposition of nature and art really misses the point, a differentiation of the two from another considera-tion (if Kant seems to have achieved the identification of the products of nature and of art in esthetic appraisal) has been rendered possible by virtue of the fact that in an esthetic evaluation nature and art are not to be differ-entiated in so far as nature ceases in the traditional concept to be nature if evaluated according to formal and logical concepts of expediency and is evaluated in analogy to the products of a reasonable being. In this case a differentia-tion between natural events and human actions becomes impossible in that it is a matter of indifference for the evaluating subject whether the expediency grasped in the esthetic appraisal of an object logically preceded the object as a conceptual pattern or not. The nature of the esthetic judgment is in no wise affected by such knowledge; it still remains only subjective with a claim to objective validity. Thus, it is really impossible for Kant to divide nature and art, be it by juxtaposition or by parallelism. In the former case, it is impossible to point to a principle which legitimizes itself on the basis of critical idealism by which a realm of art could separate out from the general field of phenomena. In the latter case it is impossible to point to a principle by which nature could be distinguished from art in an esthetic appraisal. At one time art is already included in the concept of nature in so far as it forms a constituent of the world of appearance; the next time nature is thought of in the concept of art as an object of esthetic judgment. This is patent in the final classification of the general introduction (p. 38): Nature is cited as an object of the understanding which relates to the *a priori* principle of regularity. Here nature comprises the world of appearances which actually is first created by the intuitive understanding. Thus, every type of art is also included in nature. The power of judgment, with its *a priori* principle of expediency, has reference to art according to the same classification. This classification is only justified when we understand by art the totality of all appearances to which *a priori* principles of expediency may be applied for the purpose of evaluating them. Since this applies, however, to the entire world of appearances, if one brings esthetic evaluation to bear equally upon pleasure and displeasure, the entire world of appearances is, again, included in art so that in both sides of the classification each time the same is included under a different name. Therefore, on the basis of

Kant's investigation, nature and art are completely coincident. They both designate the world of appearances as a whole, be it as a creation of our understanding, be it as an object of our judgment. The tripartite division respecting the faculty of knowledge thus arrived at is possible only by virtue of the fact that the same concept has been included twice under different names, but with the same content, for two faculties of knowledge.

By the same token, it may be shown that the field of art embraces at the same time the field of freedom, because the concept of freedom is a presupposition for the delineation of the field of art in so far as the latter, being a spontaneous happening, does not take into consideration the mechanism of nature when the possibility of appraising expediency is involved. Thus, art is already an appraisal of what is happening as taking place spontaneously. This same impossibility of making a separation in principle appears when one tests the classification in line with the *a priori* principles in that every principle of expediency, no matter what, must, if thought through all the way, lead of necessity to the idea of a final purpose to which it is oriented. This is a thought which Kant himself later incorporated as a principle in his presentation in that he has the teleological judgment attain to perfection only in moral theology. In this manner, the very same object is again included in this tripartite division under the field of freedom, as in the two first-mentioned ones. It is the world of appearances which is presented to view here in analogy to moral activity in so far as the principle of its happening was generally understood from the point of view of art.

What about the *a priori* validity of the concept of expediency in regard to an "objective" purposive evaluation? . . .

Let us take up the principal passage on p. 32 where Kant follows through with the bifurcation of judgment: "We can imagine expediency in an object given in experience for some objective reason, as agreement of the form of an object with the conceptual possibility of the thing. The concept precedes the object and contains the reason for its form."

If we consider this teleological power of judgment which judges "logically according to concepts" in all seriousness, the question will be suggested strongly to us, from where did the power of judgment get these concepts according to which it judges the real world? Whereon does its validity rest since it lays claim to general validity? If Kant had followed through with the critique of teleological judgment corresponding to this classification, he would have necessarily had to give up his conception of the *a priori* in general, in that he would have been able to base the "concepts of things which precede them and imply their form" either only on generalized experience or on an *a priori* form in Plato's sense. In doing so he would have furnished a critique of the expediency of things instead of the *Critique of Teleological Judgment,* just as he introduced a critique of taste in place of the *Critique of Esthetic Judgment.*

Now, the employment of the expression "concept" as basic to the judgment of expediency shows that Kant here operates with the terminology of ancient thought instead of with the *Critique of Pure Reason.* The ancient concept of art in sole reference to the beautiful also forces the teleological judgment of the world in the present classification (so that some relationship with the ancient concept can be established) into the ancient garb of expediency which is supported by the concept of expediency preceding the evaluation of objects. With this, Kant's formulation of the *a priori* is eliminated automatically.

Now, this unhappy description of teleological judgment on p. 32 came about only respecting the connection with the critique of taste. Just as the spell is broken, so also the Kantian interpretation of expediency throws off its ancient garb. It becomes again what it was on p. 16 ff. and seeks its foundation not upon "concepts" but on "principles." The designation of expediency as a principle becomes dominant now, and the term concept is used with the same meaning as the term principle. Specific examples may be found on p. 18. Expediency is that principle which has reference to the connection of objects themselves; hence it is not based on the expedient "concepts of these objects in so far as they precede the appraisal of them." In this rudimentary form expediency as a principle of judgment coincides with unity as a principle of grasping events in general. To that extent, expediency itself is an *a priori* principle of judgment. It is to these general ideas, not the classification on p. 32, that the *Critique of Teleological Judgment* refers, as it is developed on p. 238 ff. The views which were to make possible the classification on p. 32 disappeared without a trace. They were introduced in order to relate superficially esthetic and teleological judgment by means of the concept of expedience, which was impossible from the start in the ancient understanding of art. The investigation, henceforth, moves along the course originally plotted on p. 16 ff. This wonderful structure is thus reared which, starting with the principle of uniformity in respect to an expedient evaluation of the world, leads to the question as to the final purpose and permits teleology to fulfill itself only in an ethico-theology.

The entire *Critique of Teleological Judgment* takes its rise on Kant's original idea on p. 16 ff., and leaving out of account its formulation on p. 32 becomes intelligent right from the start as having been founded on necessity from the following observation. The reader may remember how we proved earlier that the context in which Kant's original ideas on p. 16 ff. moved has a one-sided reference to "nature" without our being able to discover a principle to distinguish art from nature. However, on p. 32 ff., the statements are made solely with a view to art, in that it is impossible to distinguish nature from art, provided one rejects the popular distinction. Thus, we have won the original concept of purpose concerning nature as nature (p. 16 ff.) and the difficulties in the concept of purpose do not arise before we meet the statement (on p. 32 ff.) that art really includes nature in itself. At the moment when nature as nature again dominates the reflection (p. 236 of the *Critique of Teleological Judgment*), the original concept of purpose likewise comes into its own and all difficulties disappear.

Thus, the *Critique of Judgment* is arranged on the broad basis of nature as nature as is shown first in the concept of expediency. Only the endeavor to fit a critique of taste into this frame as a critique of esthetic judgment resulted in the concepts in question becoming inadvertently differently oriented. This came to the fore clearly in the classification on p. 32, and may be demonstrated mainly with respect to the concept of expediency.

We have just demonstrated the consequences of this subterfuge for the validity of the "*a priori* principle" of the judgment in question and have shown how the critique of taste loses its claim to *a priori* principles by virtue of the transformation of the concept of purpose, while the *Critique of Teleological Judgment,* going back to the original formulation of that concept, is able to deduce especially from this very fact the right to carry along *a priori* principles in the judgment. With this we are forced to make a second conclusion. It has reference to the main question with respect to which the investigations thus far derive any value at all. "Does the *Critique of Judgment* perform the task which it undertakes to perform, that is, to demonstrate the connection between understanding and reason by virtue of the power of judgment?"

The question has, in principle, already been decided: The *Critique of Judgment* does not undertake a solution because it cannot by itself establish the connection between esthetic and teleological judgment, but unites both only superficially in the concept of expediency. Naturally, if one looks more closely into the formulation of the concept of expediency, the poorly concealed discrepancy reveals itself especially in the classification which Kant offers. Thus, the *Critique of Judgment* joins understanding and reason in that it carries the distinction into the power of judging itself.

This conclusion may be reached even in a purely formal way if we recall the statements made thus far concerning the significance of the feeling of pleasure and displeasure.

On the one hand, in the main passages—where it is a matter of the connection made in judgment between understanding and reason—the feeling of pleasure and displeasure respecting them is, in general, brought in relation to the power of judgment. From the start, the preparatory step taken to accomplish the connection on p. 16 is characteristic of the role which here falls to the feeling of pleasure. It is stated on p. 16: "The feeling of pleasure is lodged between the faculty to know and the faculty to desire, just as the power of judgment is lodged between understanding and reason." This recognition is, then, utilized to demonstrate as possible that the power of judgment contains a principle *a priori* and that, furthermore, through the connection of the feeling of pleasure and displeasure with the faculty of desiring, a transition may be made from the field of concepts dealing with nature to the field of the concept of freedom, which, then, makes possible the transition from understanding to reason (p. 16). Here, the core of the thinking lies in that the power of judgment as such is brought in connection with the feeling of pleasure and displeasure, because only thus can the connection with the faculty of desiring be accomplished.

Right in line with these reflections, we read next, on p. 25 ff.: "Concerning the Connection of the Feeling of Pleasure with the Concept of Expediency in Nature." What is now being discussed in regard to "nature" the main classification on p. 38 seeks to convey in regard to "art." Here also the feeling of pleasure and displeasure is brought into relation with judgment in general. In between, on p. 32, lies the classification into formal and logical expediency in which case only the former may, under reversal of the logical relationship, be brought into relation with the feeling of pleasure, while the latter, on the contrary, has to do not "with a feeling of pleasure in things, but with the understanding when we judge them." This logical judgment is attributed, on p. 33, to understanding and reason. Thus, either the concept of pleasure and displeasure conceals the imperfectly accomplished contact between esthetic and teleological judgment (cf. pp. 17 and 38), or the expression "expediency" apparently holds together esthetic and teleological judgment if one has to drop the general relationship of the feeling of pleasure in the interest of a possible classification.

Since, however, the separation continues factually as the work progresses, it is not a question of the connection between understanding and reason through the power of judgment; rather, esthetic and teleological judgment each of itself and independently of the other endeavors to establish this connection with reason without having the ability to maintain such a connection among themselves.

Should one now reflect that, according to our earlier demonstrations, an investigation of the sublime spills over the narrow framework of the critique of taste, which, therefore, independently of the latter, must establish for itself the connection in question, then the *Critique of Judgment* occupies itself with the solution of the task, generally called into being by the *Critique*, in three separate areas: How is the connection between understanding and reason to be proven scientifically (as having been accomplished by the power of judgment) by research into 1) the beautiful, 2) the sublime, and 3) teleology in general?

In the general survey of the difficulties which are founded in the plan of the *Critique of Judgment*, we have already touched upon the concept of the supersensuous. This concept plays a predominant role in the investigation concerning the sublime. This becomes apparent in the fact that of those places where the concept of the supersensuous occurs in the *Critique of Judgment*, more than half are devoted to the investigation of the sublime. The characteristic thing in the concept of the supersensuous which is related to that of the sublime is the difficulty we experience in making it coincide with the concept of the intelligible. This is attested to also by the extremely rare appearance of the concept of the intelligible. On pp. 108 and 109 we gain an insight into the difficulties. In this narrow space, the terms which we are endeavoring to equate clash with each other. Starting with a comprehension of the sublime, one arrives at the concept of the supersensuous only by detouring over the concept of the infinite. That object is sublime, and that alone, when nature as a whole is suited as a measure: "The real, unchanging, basic measure of nature is the totality of nature herself which, as phenomenon, is comprehended infinity" (p. 109).

How does one get from this concept of the absolute whole of the world of appearances (for it is only with this that we are dealing when it is being considered a measure for estimating mathematical magnitude) to the concept of the supersensuous? Kant's auxiliary idea is as follows: "Since this basic measure is a self-contradictory concept (on account of the impossibility of the absolute totality of a progress without end), it is that magnitude of an object of nature on which the imagination expends its entire faculty of comprehension fruitlessly, which must lead the concept of nature to a supersensuous substratum (which at one and the same time underlies nature and our faculty) which is great beyond all measure of sense" (p. 109). This reflection does not lead further than to the concept of a "supersensuous substratum" whose derivation proclaims itself in the contradictory statement "that it is great beyond all measure of sense." A "substratum" to which an estimate of magnitude is applied positively or negatively is, however, no longer a substratum. Thus, the flaws in the reflection show themselves in that passage where Kant undertakes to justify scientifically the equation of "nature as totality" with its "intelligible substratum" in a discussion which he already used in the *Critique of Pure Reason.*

A coalescence of the infinite with the supersensuous, apparently also a coalescence of the infinite with the intelligible (if it is a question of investigating the sublime), may be based on the impossibility of a *progressus in infinitum,* but not the identification of the supersensuous with the intelligible. Thus, in investigations of the sublime, the "supersensuous"—and not the "intelligible"—dominates one's thinking, and the attempted coalition of both which takes place on a large scale unnoticed in the *Critique of Pure Reason* when the antinomies are under discussion, . . . turns out to be infeasible in the section at hand when one consults the numerical relationship of the terms "supersensuous" and "intelligible" in researching the sublime. . . . The sublime is conjoined with reason as the faculty of progressively unifying experience up to the unattainable absolute. The supersensuous in question is both times the "totality of possible appearances," experienced at one time by virtue of the impossibility of a perfectly unified comprehension of the totality of appearances, the next time by virtue of the impossibility of applying the relative measures of magnitude and power to certain appearances. Therefore, we may say that the sublime rests on the comprehension of an appearance by reason. Consequently, it is really no longer a matter of a union of judgment and reason regarding the sublime, but both faculties of knowledge pass over into each other without distinction in this problem, as is indicated by the same subject in both cases, that is, man as moral being, and the agreement in formulation of the concept "supersensuous" in so far as it maintains contact with the concept of the infinite.

Our investigation has arrived at a decisive point: The subject of the esthetic valuation is the person. The entire thought and idea content of the person comes to the fore in a progressive crescendo when we comprehend esthetically the world of appearance, beginning with the simplest esthetic formal unity and ending in the most complicated, and apparently incomprehensible, progressive esthetic comprehension. Let this be imagined as a sort of process of empathy, or let the attempt be made to describe the process by utilizing the terms "mood" or "imagination"; the fact is well established that nature as appearance becomes art in that the person discovers within himself an idea which, related to appearance, seizes upon the principle of an esthetic unity. The process of the esthetic apprehension of a landscape, the explanation of which Kant has to forego, may, accordingly, be described in main outlines. The whole series of appearances is held together in a unity by a thought. Thus, from being an appearance, the landscape in spring becomes an object of art, as does the dreary sandy desert. These processes presuppose a personality which has developed thoughts and ideas to a significant degree of refinement. Therefore, it is explainable that in the development of mankind, as in that of the individual, not until a certain point in the development has been reached, to cite an example, does the landscape become art. Descriptions of landscape and landscape painting are relatively of recent date. It was not until the Renaissance that an esthetic apprehension of the landscape really came into being, while the ancient literature offers relatively few examples of it and leaves the esthetic evaluation of the landscape still in a certain dependence on the feelings of pleasure and displeasure relative to the pleasant and unpleasant.

It, likewise, corresponds to what has been said when each thought entering anew in the history of mankind's development manifests its influence through an enrichment of the esthetic field. Thus, the proliferation of historic insight, which places past epochs of civilizations vividly before our eyes, signifies an advancement of the esthetic comprehension of objects which otherwise would hardly be sensed as art because a multitude of historical ideas are brought to bear upon them. Thus, a heap of rubble on a mountain becomes art because around it hovers the romantic spell of the Middle Ages. At the moment when we might be convinced that it is contemporary, it would be impossible to accomplish an esthetic unity with respect to it; it would remain appearance, a picture of loathsome disorder. A couple of broken columns and a bit of blue sky and the landscape becomes art if the appraiser's memory and insight into the ancient Hellenic splendor awaken. If this is not the case, the infertile imagination cannot complete the insight, and the object remains appearance. Kant's example of the imitated song of a nightingale (p. 168) and, likewise, the example of artificial flowers transplanted into nature (p. 164) are, thus, disposed of. Why does all esthetic interest fade after the deception has been discovered? Because the person is no longer capable of comprehending the unity in the objects and their environment by bringing their ideas to bear upon them. It is no longer the melancholic, mild, moonlit summer's night which allows us to construct the song of the little bird as a harmonious unity, but it is a succession of notes which, as noise, we sense as unpleasant because we cannot accomplish a sense of oneness between it and peaceful nature.

That Kant's example is, taken by itself, correct, but the explanation of it made from the context into which it has been pressed, totally wrong, becomes clear if we undertake a modification of the example. If, for instance, one substitutes the warbling of the nightingale by a beautiful human song modulated in soft rhythms, the esthetic effect of nature is not diminished despite Kant who would not acknowledge it as nature. Rather, the esthetic effect of nature will become intensified because the appreciator can now construct once more a unity among the succession of notes, their origin and nature. However, the esthetic unity can also be constructed for the imitated bird song, as shown by Beethoven's Pastoral Symphony. The imitation of the song in this composition is not felt as a noise, but as art because it is incorporated into an esthetic unity even though only for the one who is able to accomplish the unity intended by the composer. Thus, it is demonstrated especially in the most complicated examples that nature does become art in that the person brings to bear his entire wealth of ideas and thoughts to the appearance and seizes them in an esthetic unity. The richer this content, the larger the area of art for the person who is the judge.

Thus it is the evaluating person "who enlarges our concept of nature from a mere mechanism to the concept of it as art" (*Critique of Judgment,* p. 98). On the same high level is a statement on p. 182: "The faculty of imagination (as a faculty of productive knowledge) is, it must be said, very powerful in that it creates, as it were, another nature· from the material which is presented it by the real one. We enter a discussion with her in which our experiences appear to us as commonplace; we reshape them, perchance, always, to be sure, according to the laws of analogy, yet also according to principles which are on a higher level of reason (and which come just as naturally to us as those according to which the understanding comprehends empirical nature), in which case we become aware of being free from the law of association (which is part of the empirical use of that faculty) to the end that the material may be loaned us by nature according to the law of association, but transformed by us into something else, that is, something that surpasses nature."

The principle of classification and progression in the arts, rooted in a grasp of the essence of art in its true scope, contains not only an indication of a combination of the esthetic judgment with practical reason, but, if thought through consistently, furnishes the proof for it so independently that the investigation concerning the combination in question could be terminated merely by pursuing the problem of the classification and stepwise sequence of the arts.

The second problem, which we also want to investigate in its relation to Kant's philosophy of religion, concerns the section which Kant devotes to the understanding of genius. This is, perhaps, the most unsatisfactory part of the entire *Critique of Judgment*. Here, the narrowing down process initiated by Kant's concept of art draws the ultimate conclusions. The investigation of genius extends only to art in so far as it concerns human activity. This unjustifiably constricted circle is further contracted. Genius is being investigated in its relation to the "fine arts," and of these only the graphic arts are taken into account. In this way, however, every connection between the investigation of the esthetic genius and the investigation of the nature of genius has, in general, been made impossible. Should the investigation of the esthetic genius be confined to its proper boundaries, it must take into consideration genius in its relation to its entire field of operation, the world of appearances in general. However, a principle of differentiation between the world of appearances and the field of human activity cannot, then, be discovered. The nature of genius consists, namely, in the singular crescendo of the faculty for understanding the world of appearance as art, if we define genius in connection with the main esthetic problem. Before genius becomes a cause of appearances which it manufactures in order to be judged as art, it must have understood these appearances in nature as art. The painter, before he presents a process in which the art of a genius may be sensed, must have previously understood this process as appearance by virtue of his genial talent. Thus, the artistic production is not a characteristic mark, but only a result, of genius.

Now, the occurrence of genius, in whatever art, denotes a progress in that art. Furthermore, every progress in art consists in the fulfillment of its principle of unity. Genius is, thus, characterized as a unique ability to accomplish an esthetic unity in a field of appearances at a point where it had not been accomplished up to that time, or to accomplish it in such a manner as would not be possible with the customary means of unification. In that it introduces a more perfect principle of unity into art, the genius seizes upon something as art that up to that time was mere appearance, or enhances art in such a way that the others, who are incapable of accomplishing this unity with the customary means, believe art has been reduced to appearance. Thus, it lies in the nature of genius to be misunderstood and in the nature of the progress of art (that is, the art of the genius) to be looked upon, in the average sensibility of contemporary art appreciation, as appearance. Thus, when Bach breathed into counterpoint, which in itself is an empty pattern, the idea of a unified development, by virtue of which all his works possess such a surprising perfection and unity, his music was felt, particularly by capable contemporary musicians, to be noise, and it was first Beethoven who possessed the genius to discover art in Bach. Likewise, every progress in the graphic arts, if it can be traced back to the genius of individuals, is felt by most contemporaries as a "senseless imitation or distortion of nature."

This definition of genius as the unique faculty of seizing the esthetic unity in objects leads us to recognize their connection with genius also in other fields as soon as one returns to the subject problem. The subject is the person. In so far as it has the talent to accomplish an esthetic unity, one calls it artistic genius. If it is the religious or ethical nature of the person which seizes the world of appearances and its events in a corresponding unique unity, one calls it moral or religious genius. Therefore, the nature of every religious genius is shown in that he constructs a unity by working over the wreckage of a religion destroyed either deliberately or unconsciously as the exigencies of his religious personality dictate it without concern as to whether, for the average person, the broken pieces do fit together into a structure or not. The genius seizes what is only in the light of its own converging into a unified image —and the rest becomes blurred in the shade. Thus, for Jesus of Nazareth, only that exists in the Old Testament which proves to be in harmony with his religious talent. It is from here that light is shed: "On these two hang all the law and the prophets." In this manner Augustine unites the contradictions of a Neoplatonic world view and Catholicized Christianity into one whole; he establishes the higher unity of both without feeling the contradictions. Thus Luther, being the religious genius that he was, fits together the most contradictory portions of medieval dogma because he brings a unified principle to bear on it; he voiced contradictions, but he never felt them. In every religious genius progress toward the principle of unity is documented just as in the esthetic genius. Because progress cannot be achieved on the basis of the customary or the habitual, it is especially the religiously interested masses who sense the new structure not as religion but as appearance—that is, as a conglomerate of religious pronouncements—and the religious genius becomes a deluded heretic.

In analogy to the religious genius, the moral genius likewise presents itself as the accomplishment of a higher unity in evaluating phenomena on the basis of the dominant moral determination of the person. Socrates accomplished this unity in appraising the world of appearances morally without feeling the need for extending this unity to the whole field of events and seizing as unitary all happenings in the world in a moral evaluation. Kant, too, is a moral genius like Socrates—and one of overwhelming magnitude. He is a moral genius in that he comprehends and undertakes scientific research merely for the purpose of demonstrating the reality of the moral law. At the moment when, in the development of the epistemological problem posed by Descartes, the consequences were drawn from his moral indifference—which a Spinoza could still pass over lightly—Kant, in his critical investigations, so transforms the setting and solution of the problem that it tends toward a moral interpretation of the world. The unity which he, as a moral genius, accomplished consisted in that he brought the division made by critical idealism into an intelligible and phenomenal world into a unified combination by virtue of the fact of the moral law without his noticing the divergent tendencies of these two elements and without being obliged to draw the consequence that the moral law, when incorporated into the distinction of the intelligible and what is of the nature of appearance, renders a moral appraisal of happenings impossible.

Thus, the common element of geniuses in all fields is that genius accomplishes a new unity according to the determination of its subject as a person. The ascent from the esthetic to the moral and religious genius takes place to the extent to which a person becomes a moral person and, in turn, a religious person.

With this we conclude the difficult investigation concerning Kant's *Critique of Esthetic Judgment* in its relation to his philosophy of religion. The result is, for all points in question, the same: Kant, even though without artistic ability and training, feels the union which the esthetic judgment brings about with other faculties of knowledge. Often he describes them in a very striking manner, but is able to give reasons for it at no turn of the problem because he destroys the connection between judgment in general and esthetic judgment by introducing the popular concepts of art and expediency, and furnishes, instead of the esthetic judgment, critiques of taste and of the sublime, critiques which cannot solve the problem.

With this formulation of the result the investigation can rest satisfied. It has approached the *Critique of Esthetic Judgment* for the purpose of illuminating its place in the development of Kant's philosophy of religion. However, in the analysis of the thinking which we recognized as necessary and have followed through, still another result has urged itself on us which is related to the *Critique of Esthetic Judgment*. The place of the *Critique of Esthetic Judgment* has been taken by a critique of taste, while the general introduction of the *Critique of Judgment* has delineated the area of a *Critique of Esthetic Judgment*. Here, too, the suspicion is in order that as the sketch of a philosophy of religion was inserted into a later reflection after a slight revision, thus also the critique of taste, which belongs to an earlier epoch of Kant's thinking, may have been taken up with slight revisions into the *Critique of Judgment* in place of the *Critique of Esthetic Judgment*. The original frame of thought to which this critique of taste belongs documents itself for the first time in clear outlines in the classification of judgment into an esthetic and a teleological one (p. 33). There, a view of teleological judgment is expounded according to which it is supposed to have reference to "the agreement of the form with the possibility of the thing itself, according to a concept of it which is antecedent and contains the ground of this form." The *Critique of Teleological Judgment* offered later takes no cognizance of this determination but occupies a far less developed standpoint.

Thus, at the end of this long investigation, we are face to face with an antagonism between Kant's understanding and definition of religion, on the one hand, and the concept of religion which the philosophy of religion of critical idealism has produced spontaneously, on the other.

Let us, then, close by summarizing the result of the investigation of the *Critique of Judgment* with reference to Kant's philosophy of religion.

Kant seeks to work up a connection between the understanding and the practical moral reason through esthetic and teleological judgment, presupposing their mutual independence. In spite of valuable starts, the attempt undertaken in the field of esthetic judgment miscarried because he adopted an uncritical esthetic concept of art and expediency. In the field of teleological judgment, the attempt is carried through with strict logic up to the point where the ethico-theology builds upon teleology. From hence forth the influence of the concept of the highest good, uncritical regarding the formulation of ethico-theology, asserts itself. Furthermore, Kant's attempt to erect, in the field of teleological judgment, a philosophical-religious structure is not carried out consistently to the very end because for the last part of the structure, the material which was already utilized in the sketch of a philosophy of religion and in the *Critique of Practical Reason* is again being utilized. The adoption of otherwise oriented thoughts is made possible by virtue of the fact that in some respects the moral theology transcends the rigid forms of the *Critique of Practical Reason* and, driven by moral interests, reaches back into the richer thought content of the sketch of a philosophy of religion. Once taken up, some of these thoughts can no longer be brought into relationship with moral theology, and they pass once more through the development leading to the thought structure of the *Critique of Practical Reason*. That train of thought in the sketch of a philosophy of religion which is geared to general reflections is further developed in the ethico-theology in the direction of *Religion Within the Limits of Reason Alone*. Through the concept of moral mankind as the final end of the world, we see how preparations are being made in the ethico-theology for the moral valuation of earthly conditions as good, the receding into the background of the ethical interest in the continuation of our existence, the act of relating the concept of God to the "ethical common being" and the moral concept of happiness. These magnitudes, then, lay the condition for the advancement of thought in *Religion Within the Limits of Reason Alone* in their pure formulation. Without a preceding ethico-theology, *Religion Within the Limits of Reason Alone* would be incomprehensible in the developmental process of the Kantian philosophy of religion. The ethico-theology again picks up the thoughts which the formation of the philosophy of religion of critical idealism had eliminated, in the *Critique of Practical Reason,* from the Kantian philosophy of religion. The ethico-theology gives them a more logical formulation and brings to them a deeper grasp of the moral law by which these thoughts attain an enrichment of their moral worth. However, the ethico-theology points forward to *Religion Within the Limits of Reason Alone* and backward to the sketch of a philosophy of religion. Through slight contact with the *Critique of Practical Reason,* it shows that Kant's philosophy of religion is engaged in a stage of development which presents itself as a movement away from the philosophy of religion of critical idealism. In the *Critique of Judgment,* the terms supersensuous and intelligible still struggle for equal place. In *Religion Within the Limits of Reason Alone.* the struggle has been decided in favor of the term supersensuous.

# General Summary and Conclusion

We have made our investigation in the manner projected in the general introduction in the four writings which are of special interest for Kant's philosophy of religion. Every type of reflection has been investigated by itself and only after it was thoroughly understood compared with the reflections in other writings and brought into relationship to them. Hence, in the presentation of Kant's philosophy of religion we have already prepared the solution for the problem which was broached in the introduction. It has reference to the question whether and in how far a philosophy of religion rising above the basis of critical idealism is possible.

No matter at which point the investigation starts, the result is the same: A philosophy of religion tailored and oriented to the presuppositions of critical idealism is a product which is self-disintegrating. The opposing forces are in equilibrium so long as they have not reached their full intensity; in this manner the sketch of a philosophy of religion can unite reason in its theoretical and practical use. The *Critique of Practical Reason,* however, can no longer reach the attempted union of practical and theoretical reason; the perfected philosophy of religion of critical idealism dissolves itself.

The later reflections only carry with them the debris of the burst structure of the *Critique of Practical Reason.* They are clearly distinguishable from the new thoughts expressed and resist every new attempt at joining them together. Thus, in the ethico-theology we meet a concept of the highest good which was under the influence of the *Critique of Practical Reason* and, subsequently, a concept of immortality divulging the same influence. These two foreign thoughts prevented the perfection of the ethico-theology according to the plan projected for it in the combination with general teleology. In the presentation of *Religion Within the Limits of Reason Alone* the influence of the thinking of the *Critique of Practical Reason* recedes into the background completely. The concept of immortality hardly ever occurs. The hypothetical positing of a "future life" shows that the continuation of our existence is not required by interest in an ethical perfection. The concept of a moral world and, at the same time, the idea of the highest good, have gained a relation to the moral society which does not suggest any attempt to realize these magnitudes in the intelligible field.

Thus, the *Critique of Practical Reason* forms the apex of that type of thinking in Kant's philosophy of religion which seeks its connection with the determinations and presuppositions of critical idealism. The trend toward this point is presented in the thinking of the sketch of a philosophy of religion. The trend downward from the apex is expressed in the successive retreat of the thoughts of the *Critique of Practical Reason* when presenting the ethico-theology in *Religion Within the Limits of Reason Alone.*

Thus, there exists an insoluble contradiction, traceable to its ultimate reasons, between the presuppositions of critical idealism and the fact of the moral law which renders impossible any philosophy of religion resting upon a union of these two factors in that the logical assertion of the one factor neutralizes the effect of the other. In the relationship of these two factors with respect to each other lie the two tendencies which we were able to pursue through the entire Kantian philosophy of religion.

In the final summing up we have assembled for comparative study the results of those trends of thinking in Kant's writings in which we could note the prevalence of the critical idealist factor over the moral one: It is Kant's philosophy of religion as the philosophy of religion of critical idealism. It reached its most complete formulation in the *Critique of Practical Reason* in the philosophy of religion conjoined with the thus formulated epistemological presuppositions. The contradiction asserting itself between both elements is covered up only tediously, and the fact is veiled that as soon as the intelligible and the moral world are brought in coalition, morality and the formulation of the moral law in Kant's sense cease to exist. This trend in the modern philosophy of religion is logically continued by the one who was able to develop Kant's epistemology to its ultimate implications because he did not possess Kant's moral depth: Schopenhauer. He drew the consequences which Kant was not able to draw because his gaze all the while strayed toward the fact of the moral law. Kant was not able to realize the ideas in the formulation as secured against all attacks in the transcendental hypotheses. His moral interest compels him to go beyond this formulation which, in view of critical idealism, is the most complete, whereby the ideas of the continuation of our existence and freedom no longer exhibit the correct coinage of critical idealism. It is no accident if Schopenhauer returns again and again to the transcendental hypotheses in questions involving continued existence and freedom, and starts with the *Critique* only at that point where Kant allows the fact of the moral law to enter his investigation. He completes the de-ethicalization which principally lies already in the consistency of the presentation of Kant's *Critique of Practical Reason;* he does away with the moral law in Kant's formulation, carries to completion the identification of the knowing subject with the moral person, defines the relationship between the intelligible and phenomenal world by rejecting every attempt at bringing it home in analogy to the relationship of reason and consequence, and makes no attempt to distinguish between human action and the area of general appearances. Implied in this is that, for the purpose of realizing the intelligible, it is necessary to start with a principle which, unlike the moral law in Kant, is given as related only to a definite area of appearances but is applicable to the determinations of relations between every appearance and the intelligible sphere whereby, however, the starting point may be taken solely from the knowing subject. Thus is completed the de-ethicalization of the philosophy of religion of critical idealism in Schopenhauer's theory of the will; and the moral indifference of the Occidental epistemological problem, which seemingly had been overcome by Kant, comes to the fore again at the moment when a follower of Kant who does not comprehend the ethical depth of the founder of critical idealism begins to sift the results of the *Critique of Pure Reason* and develop them logically.

This, in brief strokes, is the entire thinking of Kant's philosophy of religion. The presuppositions of critical idealism withdraw entirely into the background. Moral mankind, not the rational being, is the subject of investigation. To the extent that these presuppositions give way, the purely ethical formulation of the statements becomes more and more noticeable. The world is considered in them only as far as the moral law extends and world events and world order refer to moral mankind. The concept of God is realized with a view to the ethical community, and the subject as moral individual is considered only in his mutual relationship with this community. Immortality does not enter into this thinking. The entire thought structure culminates in the concept of God as a moral person.

Thus, each one of the two types of thinking which may be pursued in Kant's philosophy of religion forms a system of philosophy of religion by itself if taken in the context of its consequences. At the same time either the critical idealistic presuppositions neutralize their ethical determination, or the latter cancels the former. It is implied in the logical consequences of these facts that every one of these trends of thought in the course of the history of the philosophy of religion received a logical treatment, in which case the dependence on Kant, who gave it that treatment, must have been more or less present to the thinkers who pursued them.

We have arrived at the end of our investigation. The main result can be briefly formulated thus. The Kantian philosophy of religion is fulfilled in a great development which is conditioned by the relationship between two parallel ways of thinking. The philosophy of religion of critical idealism contained in the *Critique of Practical Reason* is but a stage in this development. That it no longer is able to carry out the scheme of a philosophy of religion in the transcendental dialectic proves that, impelled by the developmental principle of the Kantian philosophy of religion, it itself is in the process of transcending the limits of the area of critical idealism. The driving factor in this development is the conception of the moral law which becomes more and more profound. It is Kant's self-perfecting ethical personality which is at the root of this development. Only in this development does the wealth of thought of Kant's philosophy of religion proclaim itself. However, his thought will also be able to exercise its influence upon today's philosophy of religion when the insight attains widespread acceptance that Kant's philosophy of religion may not be expounded and evaluated solely upon the schematism of the *Critique of Practical Reason*.